Yuji Nawata, Hans Joachim Dethlefs (eds.)
Performance Spaces and Stage Technologies

Theatre Studies | Volume 146

Yuji Nawata, born in 1964, studied German Literature at the University of Tokyo, PhD 1994. Habilitation in Kulturwissenschaft (culture science) at the Humboldt-Universität zu Berlin 2011. Since 2002, he has been a Professor at the Department of German Studies of Chuo University in Tokyo. Current interest: Combining cultural history with global history.

Hans Joachim Dethlefs, born in 1952, received his doctorate from Philipps-Universität Marburg and works as a professor at the Department of German Studies at Chuo University, Tokyo. Publications, among others, include the following: "Der Wohlstand der Kunst: Ökonomische, sozialethische und eudämonistische Sinnperspektiven im frühneuzeitlichen Umgang mit dem Schönen" (Tokyo 2010). His research focuses on the evolution of Northern European art terminologies following Italian art theory.

Yuji Nawata, Hans Joachim Dethlefs (eds.)
Performance Spaces and Stage Technologies
A Comparative Perspective on Theatre History

[transcript]

Bibliographic information published by the Deutsche Nationalbibliothek
The Deutsche Nationalbibliothek lists this publication in the Deutsche Nationalbibliografie; detailed bibliographic data are available in the Internet at http://dnb.d-nb.de

© 2022 transcript Verlag, Bielefeld

All rights reserved. No part of this book may be reprinted or reproduced or utilized in any form or by any electronic, mechanical, or other means, now known or hereafter invented, including photocopying and recording, or in any information storage or retrieval system, without permission in writing from the publisher.

Cover layout: Maria Arndt, Bielefeld
Cover illustration: Stagehands with candles shine light onto the faces of Kabuki actors. In: RYÛTEI Tanehiko (text) / UTAGAWA Kunisada (illustrations): »Shôhon jitate gonichi no ezôshi«, Edo (today's Tokyo) 1816. From the collection of the Art Research Center, Ritsumeikan University (Kyoto, Japan). Article No.: hayBK03-0543-01. The original illustration spans two full pages; for the cover of this book, it was trimmed and the empty space between the verso and recto pages was omitted.
Printed by Majuskel Medienproduktion GmbH, Wetzlar
Print-ISBN 978-3-8376-6112-5
PDF-ISBN 978-3-8394-6112-9
https://doi.org/10.14361/9783839461129
ISSN of series: 2700-3922
eISSN of series: 2747-3198

Printed on permanent acid-free text paper.

Contents

Preface
NAWATA Yuji and Hans Joachim DETHLEFS 7

**Performance Spaces in Ancient Chinese Cities:
Street Theatres of the 9th Century Capital Chang'an**
SEO Tatsuhiko 13

The Semi-Circular Theatre in Seleucid and Arsacid Babylon
MITSUMA Yasuyuki 33

**The Perspectival Stage in Sebastiano Serlio's *Second Book
of Architecture* (1545) and its German Reception in the Context
of *Wohlstand***
Hans Joachim DETHLEFS 47

**Central Perspective in Catholic Churches and on Stage in Europe
between the 15th and 17th Centuries**
ISHIDA Yuichi 91

Notable Spectacles in the Late 19th-Century Kabuki Stage
HIOKI Takayuki 103

Berlin and its Theatres between 1870 and 1890
ITODA Soichiro 111

**The Theatres in Modern Shanghai:
From the Perspective of Cultural History**
ENOMOTO Yasuko 123

Discussions on Theatre Spaces and Theatre Materials by the Leningrad School
ITO Masaru 133

Projection Technology and the Theatre Stage: Light, Space, Body Politics
Kai VAN EIKELS 143

Cultural Techniques of Play: A Global Perspective
NAWATA Yuji 157

Contributors 171

Preface

NAWATA Yuji and Hans Joachim DETHLEFS

The research project titled 'Towards a Global History of Culture' at Chuo University, Tokyo, examines cultural history from a global perspective, with theatre as a point of interest. A symposium dedicated to this topic was supposed to be held at our institution in March 2020 titled 'Theatre History as a History of Performance Spaces and Stage Technologies: A Comparative Perspective'.

However, the pandemic prevented the event from coming to fruition. Since the researchers were unable to gather and exchange thoughts in a physical place, they had at least two alternatives: meet in virtual space such as Zoom and/or to condense their ideas into an extremely small (or electronic) space known as an (e-)book and offer it for public discussion. We have chosen the second option, and hence, this was how the present volume came into being.

Theater, art, literature, religion, law, urbanism, architecture, technology—this is an interdisciplinary book that discusses the histories of these fields in various ways. Geographically, it covers a significant portion of the globe; chronologically, it ranges from ancient times to the present. We hope that readers who specialize in different disciplines, regions, and periods will be interested in this book. The broad spectrum of contributions gathered here may present a challenge to the reader, which is why the editors thought it useful to provide a brief summary in advance.

(1) SEO Tatsuhiko's contribution deals with street theater in Chang'an, the capital of the Tang Dynasty in early 9th century China with a population of approximately 700.000. The high level of urbanization, expansion of monetary economy, and international trade relations led to functional differentiations and consequently, to the construction of an international cultural metropolis in which a variety of religious denominations became indigenous, including Buddhism, Taoism, Manichaeism, Christianity, and

Zoroastrianism. This mixed culture left its mark on contemporary street theater. Seo analyzes a play performed in the streets and recorded as *The Tale of Li Wa*, which shows the urban structure of Chang'an and can be considered one of the earliest love stories in eastern Eurasia.

(2) MITSUMA Yasuyuki deals with the semicircular ancient theater built and rebuilt in the Greek or Roman style in Babylon, the ancient central city of Babylonia, at the time of the Seleucid and Arsacid dynasties (305/304 – 141/140 BC and 141/140 BC – 224 AD, respectively). The theater not only functioned as a playground for Greek tragedies but also as a meeting house for the Greco-Macedonian resident group and a place for political propaganda toward this group.

(3) The perspective in Italian Renaissance stage was codified by Sebastiano Serlio; his theatrical treatise from the *Second Book of Architecture* (1545) is based on relevant passages by Vitruvius on Roman theater. Both texts were translated into German by W.H. Ryff in 1547 – 48. Hans Joachim DETHLEFS describes how closely Ryff's *Vitruvius Teutsch* follows the terminology of Serlio, who translates Vitruvius's term *Scaenographia* to "perspective" and uses it as a visual guidance directed toward a vanishing point. In closed, roofed perspective theater, all spatial positions are fixed, especially those of the spectator. The linear perspective spatial calculus marginalizes vagrant gazes, movements, and interactions. Vitruvius's term, which defines ancient participatory spectator behavior in public places, is underexposed: *statio*. The term is of military origin ("stationing"); Vitruvius describes a (collective) pause at cultic places that correspond to the statio of the stars, i.e., the periodic return of the stars to the starting point of their courses. However, the actual orientation of the crowd was with regard to the statio principis, i.e., the position of Augustus, to whom the ten architectural books are dedicated. Ryff translates the term "statio" to "Stellung" or to "stand," which aims at controlling the public space according to respective social rank. An example of theatricality in a public setting outside a theater building is the anatomical theater, first depicted on the frontispiece of Andreas Vesalius's seminal Fabrica (1543). In this occupation-related theater, the communicative behavior of participants (in relation to the ancient statio) is expressed clearly.

(4) ISHIDA Yuichi examines how Andrea del Pozzo uses the term *theatrum* in his *Perspectiva pictorum et architectorum* (1693) to describe the "Wedding at Cana" in the Gesù Church in Rome as a setting where he decorated the high altar to bring a religious miracle to life for the audience (congrega-

tion) in visual fusion. The Jesuit Pozzo presents clear rules of perspective for the construction of scenes. Ishida analyzes the usage of the term theatrum at that time and states that it referred to both settings for church ceremonies and stages for theatrical performances in the modern sense.

The following three contributions deal with international entertainment culture around 1900.

(5) HIOKI Takayuki is devoted to the Kabuki theater of the late Tokugawa period and the Meiji era (in the second half of the 19th century to the early 20th century according to the Christian calendar), specifically to questions surrounding stage props for realistic performances of disasters and battle scenes, such as the use of magic lanterns or gunpowder. Inspirations and materials were provided by real events, such as the Ansei Tokai and the Ansei Nankai earthquake (both 1854), the Boshin war (1868 – 1869), the Satsuma Rebellion (1877), the First Sino-Japanese War (1894 – 95), or the Russo-Japanese War (1904 – 5).

(6) ITODA Soichiro demonstrates how the number of theaters in Berlin in the 1870s and 1880s first increased and then decreased. He analyzes this in the context of the history of laws governing the theater: The 1869 law on the "right of unrestricted commerce" deprived court theaters of their privileges and allowed the proliferation of commercial theaters in Berlin. This law also allowed theaters and pubs to merge, causing security problems. Consequently, theaters were subject to new regulations. The time had come for artistic performances to be staged in fireproof buildings, clearly differentiated from non-theaters.

(7) ENOMOTO Yasuko examines the history of the Lyceum Theatre in Shanghai, which was founded in 1866 and was the city's first foreign theater. In 1842, after the Treaty of Nanking between Britain and Qing China opened the port of Shanghai to Western countries, it became a cosmopolitan city with the International Settlement and French Concession. The Western-style Lyceum Theatre was a venue for Westerners to perform Western works and for Westerners to watch them, but it also became a place for Chinese and Japanese audiences to experience Western culture.

The next two contributions are devoted to theater developments in the 20th century.

(8) ITO Masaru uses the example of the Leningrad School to examine the reformation of theater practice in 1920s Russia with the emergence of directors. Gvozdev and his colleagues positioned contemporary theater in a historical context to work out the possible implications of future issues. Accordingly, new theater ideas should also, especially, be inspired by historical studies. To put it another way: Ito's essay is a scientific–historical study of how theatrical space and objects on stage were thematized by the Leningrad School.

(9) Kai VAN EIKELS first traces the history of how the stages and auditoriums of European theaters have been lit or darkened, and how film screenings have been integrated into theatrical performances. Van Eikels then analyzes the various ways in which projection technologies have been used in modern theater. Examples include Robert Lepage's adaptations of Shakespeare's *Hamlet* (1995 in Toronto and 2016 in Singapore), the performances of the Japanese collective Dumb Type, such as *OR* (France, 1997), and Frank Castorf's stage adaptation of Dostoevsky's novel *Humiliated and Insulted* (Berlin, 2001). In the last example, Bert Neumann's stage set is analyzed in opposition to Peter Brook's "empty stage."

(10) The volume concludes with Nawata's contribution, which explores the concept and method of the book and attempts to sketch how some so-called cultural techniques of the theater spread globally in the history. He divides them into three categories: (1) Performance space: Nawata relies on Christopher Balme for this notion (2) Stage technology (3) The writing surface on which the plot or text of the play is written, stored, and distributed. Of these three, the first two are discussed in this book.

When writing Japanese and Chinese names, the surname is first presented, and, in certain cases, the entire surname is capitalized. In alphabetic Japanese, when two consecutive morae have the same vowel, three options are available, namely, (a) use the circumflex for long vowels ("ôzora") and do not use a circumflex (b) "ozora" or rarely use "oozora" (c). In this article, we followed methods (a) in the majority of cases and (b) for internationally used alphabetical place names, such as Tokyo, and names of contributors.

Acknowledgments

The English translations of the Japanese or German manuscripts and the proofreading of these manuscripts were mainly conducted by Ms. HIYAMA Misa, Enago and Textworks Translations.

We offer our special thanks to Ms. Hiyama, the above mentioned companies, and also the staff of Chuo University, especially Prof. AKIYAMA Yoshimi (previous director of the Institute of Cultural Sciences), Mr. HAYASHI Kazuo (head of the Research Institute's Administration Office), and Ms. KITAZAWA Maiko and Mr. MATSUI Hideaki, both who work at the same office. Without their help, the publication of this book would not have been possible.

Tokyo, July 2021
Nawata Yuji and Hans Joachim Dethlefs

Performance Spaces in Ancient Chinese Cities: Street Theatres of the 9th Century Capital Chang'an[1]

SEO Tatsuhiko

Introduction

This article aims to analyze the composition and structure of street theaters in Chang'an, the capital of the Tang Dynasty in the early 9th century, mainly based on the novel *The Tale of Li Wa* (李娃伝). *The Tale of Li Wa* is a love story written by Bai Xingjian, a scholar-official; however, it was adapted from a street play performed by wandering entertainers in Chang'an (Seo 1987b: 476-505). *The Tale of Li Wa*, the novel version of the street drama, was edited into Taiping Guangji, volume 484 published at the end of 10th century. I want to look at the street performance and theatrical presentation born in Chang'an in the 9th century through the lens of *The Tale of Li Wa*.

Behind the birth of this street love drama is the social transformation of the capital in the 9th century. Chinese society was encouraged by urbanization's progress and promoted the penetration of the monetary economy, the expansion of the commercial scale, and the complication of commercial organizations between the 9th and 12th centuries (Seo 2019a: 126-143). As a result, it increased the distribution density of human resources and materials nationwide, and promoted the common people's remarkable rise, mainly in cities. A unique urban popular culture began to develop in major cities in the Tang dynasty. Chang'an grew into a large city with about 700,000 people in the 8th and 9th centuries, becoming one of the world's largest cities at that time (Seo 2019c: 96-163).

---

1 This chapter is newly written based on the following previously published articles by Seo (1987b; 2003; 2019a; 2019b; 2019c; 2020).

Chang'an laid the foundation for national rituals and bureaucracy as the emperor's political capital and his officials. It was also a city where ancient traditional ideas intersected with the latest academic and literary trends. The new culture such as fashion, food, and music from Western countries, quickly became popular (Picken 1981-2000). Huge palaces and elaborately designed mansions of officials and merchants lined up, and it was also the center of art, where high-quality crafts, paintings, and books, including printed products, were produced (Seo 2004: 1-42). Chang'an was an international cultural city with a variety of religious faiths, including Buddhism, Taoism, Manichaeism, Christianity, and Zoroastrianism (Seo: 2019b: 1-20).

At the same time, Chang'an had a huge non-bureaucratic population and accumulated commercial wealth as a capital city. It was a city of daily encounters between people of different origins and classes. Various folk performing arts, including street performances, have been developed since the 8th century (Ditter 2011: 62-83; Shields 2014: 107-131).

Such cultural development in Chang'an is also related to the transformation of the urban social structure. Chang'an's traditional city plan was divided into symmetrical residential zones, as shown in Figure 1 (Seo 2020: 182-228). With the Daming Palace's construction in northeastern Chang'an in 663, and the new Xingqing Palace's in the eastern part in 714, the well-proportioned city plan had begun to crumble by the 8th century. As the city population and commerce activation expanded along the traffic trunk line, running east and west through the capital, the bureaucratic district formed on the hillside in the east of the city, and the common people's district formed in the western lowland areas (Seo 1987a: 159-200). The East City and its surrounding area, located in the center of the bureaucracy district, formed the city center of Chang'an by accumulating information and financial institutions. This area is the place where delicate and gorgeous crafts and sophisticated literary works could be produced. On the other hand, the popular culture was developed with the formation of the foreigners' quarter, merchants' district, slums, and settlements for people belonging to the lower hierarchy in the western city. The functional differentiation of settlements progressed in the 9th century, as shown in Figure 2 (Seo 2019c: 167-269).

Performance Spaces in Ancient Chinese Cities   15

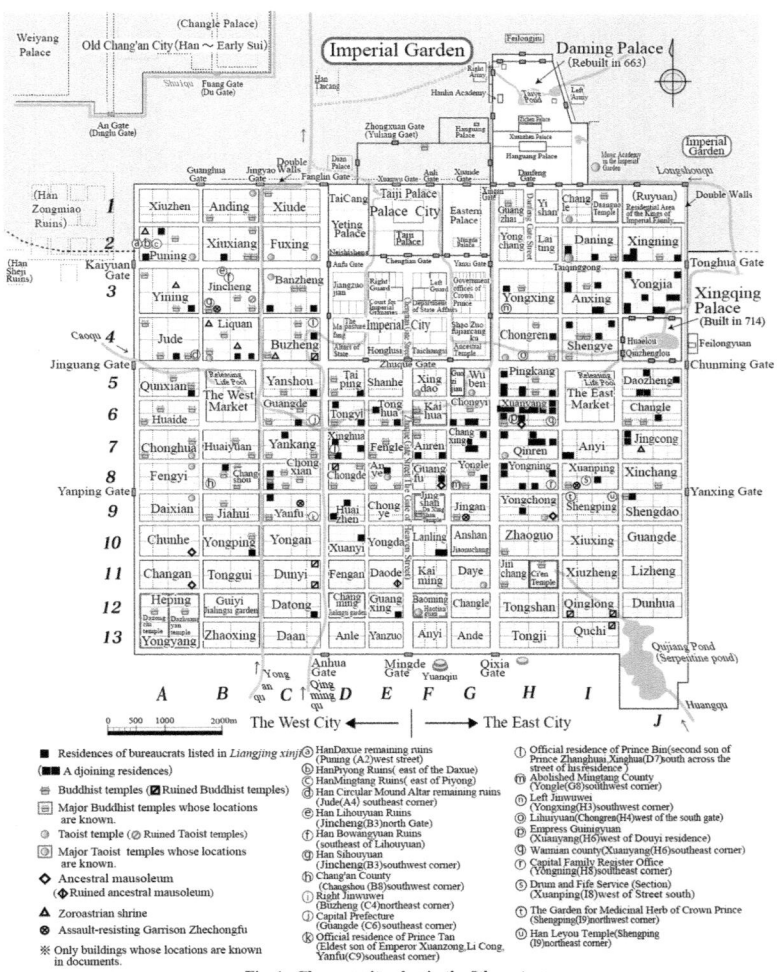

Fig. 1 Changan city plan in the 8th century
Source: Seo (2020 : 206)

16   SEO Tatsuhiko

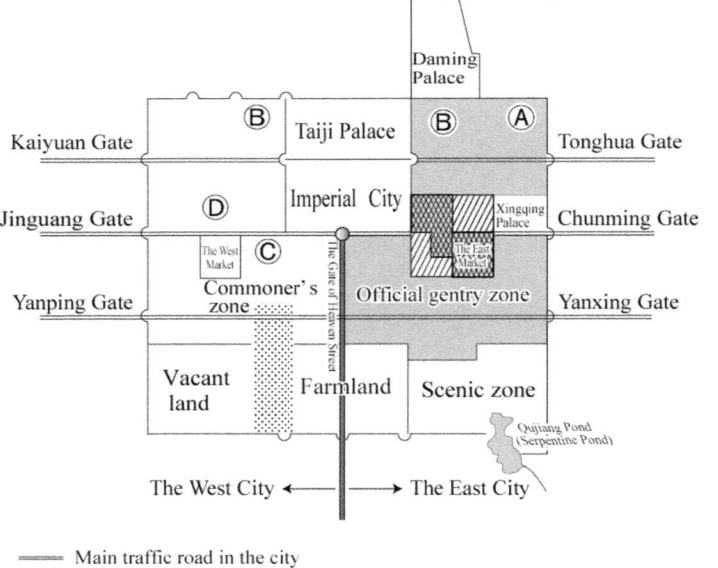

====== Main traffic road in the city
○   Stage of the song battle of *the Tale of Liwa*
        Official gentry zone
        City center (commercial, financial, and information centers)
             Pleasure quarter (The East Market, the Pingkang ward, and the Chongren ward)
        Villa area (mainly owned by senior bureaucrats living in the East City)
Ⓐ   Prince ward
Ⓑ   Eunuch residences
Ⓒ   Gathering area of bureaucrats and rich people in the West City
Ⓓ   Foreigners' quarter

Fig. 2   Functional differentiation of Changan in the 9th century
Source: Seo (2019c : 240)

1. Street Theatres in Chang'an in the 9th Century: Focusing on the Drama of The Tale of Li Wa

The Tale of Li Wa was written in the literary language by a scholar-official in the 9th century. The story was based on a musical drama performed by entertainers in the mansion in the East City of Chang'an. It was changed into a didactic story based on the scholar-official's Confucian values and differs from the composition and structure of the play when performed on a street corner (Nienhauser 2007: 91-110). It seems possible to explore the actual situation of street drama using the novelization of Li Wa's Tale as a clue.

When you read *The Tale of Li Wa*, you will notice that the names of Chang'an's street corners and walled wards appear frequently. The place names are closely connected with the story structure (Seo 1987b 476-505; Tang 2010: 113-138; Feng 2011a: 27-44). The story is designed for people who are familiar with the urban space of Chang'an. This may be related to the fact that this novel is based on a street drama that was actually performed on the streets of Chang'an. Fig. 3 shows the spaces and stages that appear in *The Tale of Li Wa*. The contents of the novel are summarized as follows (Seo 1987b 477-479; Dudbridge 1983: 104-186).

During the Tianbao reign (742–756) of the Tang Emperor Xuanzong (685-762), a prestigious son of a local official in the Lower Yangzi Delta went to Chang'an, the capital of the Tang dynasty, to take the civil examination. He stayed at an inn in the Buzheng ward (Fig.3 C4) in the West City. One day, he went to the East Market in the East City, and on the way back, entered the east gate of the Pingkang ward (H5). While traveling to visit his friends on the corner of the southwest part of the ward, he saw a beautiful courtesan, Li Wa, when he traveled through Mingke (Jingling Harness) Lane. He fell in love at first sight and returned to the inn in the Buzheng ward. His friends said that she was one of Chang'an's most reputed courtesans. He visited Li Wa's home with a large amount of money, and he greeted Li Wa's foster mother and began to live with her.

Li Wa and he lived happily, but the foster mother began telling Li Wa to leave when his money was exhausted as it slowly dwindled day-to-day. One day he and Li Wa decided to pray to the god of childbirth for a child to be born. On their way home, Li Wa abandoned him at the mansion of Li Wa's aunt near the north gate of the Xuanyang ward (H6), and no matter how much he looked for Li Wa, he was unable to find her due to the elaborate "house-moving trick" of Li Wa's foster mother and aunt. He was exhausted and returned to his former inn in the Buzheng ward in the West City. He was sick with grief, and the owner of the inn, who took care of him initially, finally left him at a funeral parlor in the West City. However, his illness healed with the help and support of the people at the funeral parlor. The man learned funeral elegies and became the best singer in the city.

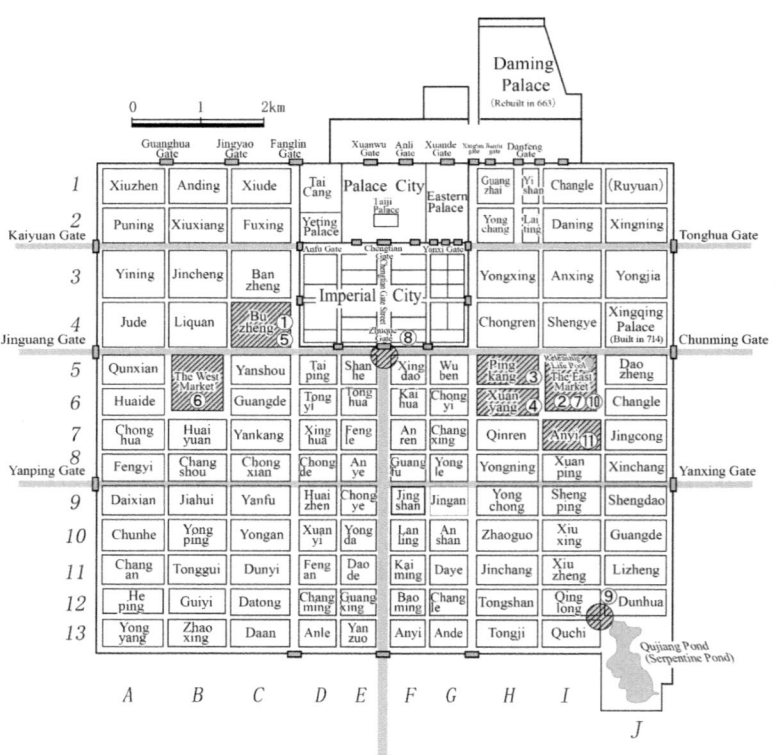

Fig. 3 Spaces and stages that appear in *the Tale of Li Wa*

①-⑪ shows stages of *the Tale of Li Wa*

Source: Seo (1987b : 478)

At the time, funeral parlors in the East and West Markets of Chang'an had ceremonial competitions. The funeral accessories and carriages of the East Market were superior to the West Market, but they were inferior in funeral elegies. Therefore, the master of the funeral parlor in the East Market secretly hired him away from the West Market funeral parlor with 20,000 in cash. The competition between the two parlors took place on the Gate of Heaven Street, located between the west and the east cities, and the loser would pay for all the costs of the food and drink for the banquet after the competition. A large crowd gathered from across Chang'an to see the exhibitions and song competitions of the funeral parlors. Before the eyes of a large crowd gathered from all around Chang'an, the funeral parlor in the East Market won the singing battle because of his talent for singing lamentations.

However, his father, who had happened to come to the capital, was among the audience. When father and son met face to face, the father was angry that he had abandoned his original purpose of passing the civil examination and brought disgrace upon his family name. He took his son around the Qujiang Pond (the Serpentine Pond) and the Apricot Orchard, located in the southeast part of Chang'an, beat him with a horsewhip, and left him for dead. Friends from the funeral parlor in the east who had followed him attempted to bury his body but found that he was breathing faintly. They brought him back to the funeral parlor, but he did not recover sufficiently and was eventually abandoned.

He dragged his purulent body and became a beggar walking around the East Market and the East City's residential area. On a snowy day, in front of a house in the Anyi ward (I7), he was nearly dead because of cold and hunger. Unexpectedly, however, the house was the one Li Wa lived in with her foster mother. Hearing the voice begging in the street, Li Wa recognized him, ran outside, and embraced him, wrapping him in a cotton garment. The two rented a new house in the northern corner of the Anyi ward (I7) and began to live together again. He passed the civil examination with top marks and subsequently passed the Plain Speech and Extreme Criticism examination and Li Wa's help. He was appointed administrator in Chengdu's higher prefecture, where he reunited with his father, who was Prefect of Chengdu. The father allowed his son to marry Li Wa. Their children are all said to have become high-ranking government officials. As summarized above, the story development of *The Tale of Li Wa* is closely linked to the urban space of Chang'an. This story is set across the entire city of Chang'an and embraces people of all social classes living in the capital (Seo 1987b: 476-505). Let's look back on the story, paying attention to the relationship between urban space and the story's development as follows (see Fig.4).

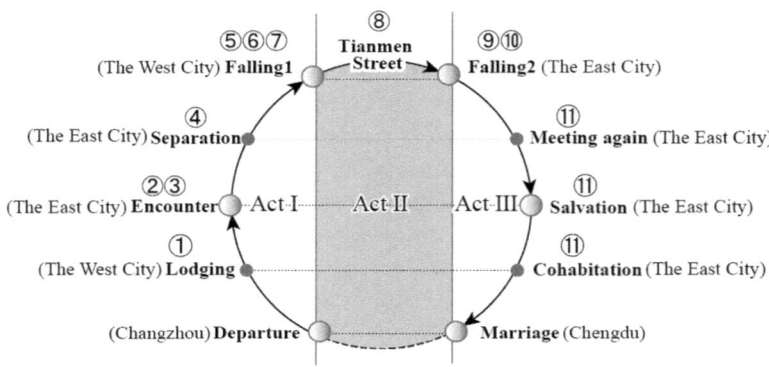

Fig.4 Structure of *the Tale of Li Wa*

① – ⑪ Story stages in Fig.3
Source: Seo (1987b : 483)

Firstly, the wealthy male embarks on a journey to the capital of Chang'an from Changzhou, located in the Yanzi Delta, which was developing at the time (**Departure**). He stays in the prosperous Buzheng ward (C4) in the West City of Chang'an (**Lodging**). Buzheng ward (C4) was the southwestern portion of the huge Imperial City, symbolizing the capital's political power, and was the northeastern part of the West City. This was a prime location in the West City along the main routes that extended outside the capital and was in a privileged living environment with culverts running north and south. This ward was also a foreign settlement. There was a Zoroastrian temple in the southwest corner of the ward. Using Buzheng ward as the stage for the introductory part of the story is intended to impress the reader because the male has entered the urban world of the imperial capital Chang'an, one of the biggest cities of the 9th century.

Secondly, the male goes to the East Market and meets Li Wa in Mingke Lane of Pingkang ward (H5). The house of Li Wa on the corner of the narrow lane is elegantly decorated. Her house has a gorgeous guesthouse and a pretty west hall with a bedroom. The tea sets and drinking vessels used for entertainment, the bedroom, curtains, and furnishings set up in the west hall, the dressing table and candles on the side of the bed, and the delicious food served by candlelight — these all imply the atmosphere of a polished culture that exists in this corner of town. A bewitching beauty, Li Wa, is at the center of the house. In other words, the movement from the inn of the West City to the East City is the move to the refined, brilliant, and sophisticated urban center. The appearance of a courtesan, Li Wa, who symbolizes the charm of the land, initiates the beginning of the story (**Encounter**).

The story begins in the East City, and the place and the behavior of the male protagonist evolve, as shown in Figure 3. However, the man, who had run out of money and been deceived and abandoned by Li Wa, was expelled from the society in the East City (**Separation**) and simultaneously thrown into the West City's lower society (**Fall 1**). Following this, the man escapes from this state of asphyxia with the help of friends from the funeral parlor. While working at funeral ceremonies in the vigorous and chaotic West City, through his education and talent acquired in his childhood, he is reborn as the best elegy singer in the capital.

After being poached by the East Market's funeral parlor, he enters the singing contest of the Gate of Heaven Street (Tianmen Street), the turning point of the story (**Gate of Heaven Street**). This is when the story turns back in the second half, and his father beats him near the Serpentine Pond (Qujiang Pond). Then, after becoming a beggar because of a fall worse than the first (Fall 2), he reunites with Li Wa (**Meeting again**) and is eventually revived as a member of the literary society in the East City when he passes the civil examination (**Salvation**). The locations of the encounter and salvation are in the same East City. However, contrary to the male's gestures and costumes that blend with the prime and bureaucratic areas of the East City in the scene of encounter, the man with the purulent body, whose temporary dwelling is a place for human and livestock dung, is forced to wander around the glamorous East Market and the bureaucratic mansion while begging until he reunites with Li Wa. The man's misery is evident; this is his condition when Li Wa runs up to him and covers him in her cotton garment. His hunger and cold finally abate, and the end of this long, rugged story is revealed (**Cohabitation**).

As mentioned above, at the starting point and turning point of the story, the actual names of the wards and the streets of Chang'an appear, providing a sense of realism. Also, because of Chang'an's urban spaces' functional differentiation in the latter half of the Tang dynasty, a specific place name evokes a specific image, making the wards and streets evocative settings for the story.

Additionally, the change of the ward name corresponds to the change of the storyline. In many cases, the choice of the ward as the stage must be deeply tied to the characters' gestures and conversations, the residence, furniture, costumes, and the like.

Such an arrangement, in which the street corners of Chang'an frequently appear and the street corner setting prepares the story's development, closely relates to the fact that a storyteller originally played the story on the streets of Chang'an. In other words, it is said that *The Tale of Li Wa*, based on a folk love drama, was written by a scholar-official, who passed the civil examination in 807, and was much too long to be told and played in one night. There are various theories about when it was documented, but they agree that it was written in the early 9th century (Seo 1987b: 482). In other words, *The Tale of Li Wa* is a work that officials transcribed in Chinese writing based on the longform oral story played by a storyteller on the street corners of Chang'an in the early 9th century.

It was inevitable that values based on Confucianism, which cultured persons at the time shared, came to the forefront when the writers recorded the story. For this reason, the work seems to have been given specific meaning by the Confucian moral view of the officials, who honor Li Wa as a remarkable woman and a wise wife. The story's main subject is Li Wa and her ethical behavior, reflected in the title, *The Tale of Li Wa*. Furthermore, at the beginning, as well as the end, of *The Tale of Li Wa*, the author notes significantly that, despite her status as a prostitute, there are rare and modern ways of doing so. The emphasis is on the man's success thanks to Li Wa's mental and material help, and his entering the civil society at the time (Seo 2003: 695-722; Tsai 2004: 99-127; Feng 2015; Luo 2015).

Although the story's narrative origin is not evident in the existing text, it was first spoken and played among the people on the street. Today's written text contains the same values as the clerk who wrote it, is an extremely compressed version of the spoken content, and suffers technical problems of writing colloquial words mixed with songs. Moreover, it is thought that the emphasis was different in many ways. The main characters in the narrative story were a female heroine and a male hero. In other words, as can be seen from *The Tale of Li Wa* and the previously-cited summaries of the text, along with the richly groomed and honored woman, the former courtesan Li Wa, the male protagonist, traverses social environments quite different from Chang'an's streets. His status declines from being an elite officer candidate, who was expected to pass the civil examination to a beggar on the roadside and is eventually rescued by a woman.

The Tale of Li Wa is a story of a wandering holy aristocrat, with a plot structure that many stories have in common. Namely, the hero's departure → 1. a fateful encounter → 2. fall of the hero → 3. salvation by the female protagonist→ 4. marriage. It is based on a popular motif of wanderers' salvation thanks to the pure love of a girl (Hashimoto 1983: 471-484; Seo 1987b: 476-505). Also, The Tale of Li Wa features the "hero's journey" trope, involving a hero who encounters various trials while wandering and traveling through different worlds. The first and second halves of the story are overturned, and as the themes of the first half of the story are denied and opposed, the second half of the narrative is completed. That is, as shown in Fig. 4 on the left, the hero's departure and marriage, the encounter with the female protagonist, and the salvation by her are paired. Additionally, in the scene with the song competition in the Gate of Heaven Street, sandwiched between two falls, the story is divided into the first and second halves, and in the latter half, the wandering circle is closed in bliss in the reverse order of the first half.

For example, although the hero's two falls before and after the Gate of Heaven Street scene seem to be the same concerning the darkness of the situation, they correspond strictly in composition and are in opposition. The story's settings change from the West City society to the East City society. The person who triggers the protagonist's fall changes from Li Wa's aunt to the protagonist's father. The character who watches the protagonist's suspended state initially and his abandonment at the end changes from the innkeeper in the Buzheng ward (C4) in the West City to the protagonist's former friends at the funeral parlor in the East City. After escaping his state of asphyxia, the protagonist changes in one instance from a civil examination candidate to a premiere funeral singer of the capital, and in the next from a singer to a beggar of the residential district of the East City. Finally, his rescuer, who allows his rebirth, changes from the funeral parlor's friends to Li Wa herself. In each case, the fall becomes more severe, and thus the final relief by Li Wa is designed to be more dramatic and significant.

2. Street Theatres in Chang'an

A festival in the Gate of Heaven Street exists as a bridge between those conflicting situations, and the scene in the Gate of Heaven Street is the turning point in the whole story, as shown in Figure 4. As an important factor that established the development of motifs in society at the time, the wards and streets of Chang'an are used. The story evolves along with the protagonist's tour of the urban space of Chang'an. Therefore, by analyzing the scenes of Chang'an as costumes that cover motifs, it is possible to discover in reverse the differences and characteristics of the motifs themselves in a particular era or region. Correlated with them, this will offer some clues to the emergence of an early Chang'an urban society.

In the 9th century, people watched various folk performing arts on the street of Chang'an. For example, in the precincts and gates of Cien Temple (H11), Qinglong Temple (J8), Jianfu Temple (F6), and Yongshou Temple (G8), there were permanent playgrounds crowded with spectacle huts where thousands could gather. In addition to the limited theaters, performances presented on the street could be seen in various places in the city. From the end of the 7th century to the beginning of the 8th century, religious music was performed on temporary stages in the streets and markets of Chang'an until dawn, and there was a report to the throne that prohibited performing music in the streets and markets in 843. Although it was not a street performance, in the early 8th century in the Liquan ward (B4), Westerners from Central Asia were seen dancing in the city's streets. There is a story of a father and daughter who walked and begged on the East City street corner, while the daughter sang a song with her father. The General of the Zhaoguo ward (H10) heard the song and her beautiful voice echoing on the street, eventually making her a concubine during the Dali year (776-79).

From the 8th and 9th centuries, folk music was introduced to rural areas by traveling entertainers, and some monks traveled around the provinces and told Buddhist tales and female actors walked and performed Buddhist drama. It is said that the origin of the folk drama, Buddhist narrative, comes from the practice of explaining Buddhism using pictures by popular artists. Since the middle of the Tang, folk poetry and songs, which had been actively conducted at each temple in Chang'an, had further advanced techniques such as Buddhist pictorial scrolls and storytelling. Folk poetry and songs, which were popular in civil society, were eventually sublimated by literati's sophisticated writings, creating new genres in the late Tang literature (Edwards 1938; Campany 2015; Mair 1997; Mair 1983).

It is thought that the storytelling that became the basis of the novel *The Tale of Li Wa* was formed during the process of popularization of prevalent performing arts since the mid-Tang. It is suggestive that, as a storytelling form, sutra-based ballads accompanied by music in medieval Japan were played by wandering groups, who are thought to have been low-ranking people who traveled across the land. Perhaps, even in Chang'an, such entertainment groups sang on street corners, competing with each other in skill and polishing their art on the playgrounds inside the temple precincts and on the streets. These were probably manifested in the prototype of *The Tale of Li Wa*. You can get a glimpse of the flow of the popular culture that matured in the Chang'an cityscape of the late Tang in the Gate of Heaven Street scene, where the protagonist was in between his falls, as shown in Table 1.

Table 1a: Comparison of the Song Battle of the Gate of Heaven Street

	Organizer	
Contrast points	*Funeral parlor of the West Market*	*Funeral parlor of the East Market*
Funeral equipment	Carriages and hearses are inferior to those of the East City.	Everyone is clean with nearly no enemy.
Stage equipment	Layer couch	Consecutive couch
Place	South corner	North corner
Singer appearance	A long-bearded man	Black turban boy
Singer props	Hold a bell and proceed	Come with a large wooden fan
Supporting role	Escort several people	Several people in the left and the right
Song of the funeral elegy	Song of the White Horse	Song of the Dew on the shallots

Table 1b: Comparison of the Song Battle of the Gate of Heaven Street

	Organizer	
Contrast points	*Funeral parlor of the West Market*	*Funeral parlor of the East Market*
Singer's gesture	Flourishing his whiskers, raising his eyebrows, clasping his wrist and inclining his head, he mounted the platform and sang the poem of the White Horse. Relying on his earlier superiority, he glanced from left and right as if no-one else came near him. He felt that he stood in a class…	Up came a youth in a black cap, who was flanked by five or six attendants holding a funeral banner. He put his clothing in order and, most deliberate in bearing, stretched out his throat. delivered a phrase of song, and looked as through he could not win. Then he…
Singer's gesture	…of his own among his contemporaries and could not be brought low.	…sang the verse "'Dew on the shallots'." His voice rose clear and penetrating, -suche that 'the echoes shook the forest trees'. "
Audience reaction	With one voice they acclaimed him.	Before the tune was finished his listeners were sobbing and sniffing as they hid tears.

Note: This table was organized with reference to the English translation of *The Tale of Liwa* by Dudbridge (1983).

Considering the examples of *The Tale of Li Wa* and the genealogy of stories that originated in the 9th century, street drama seems to have some basic elements, as I will explain in the next section.

3. Basic Structure of the Love Story: The Motif of a Man or Woman Saved or Destroyed by Love

The Tale of Li Wa is based on the universal and mythical narrative pattern of "the structure in which a male is rescued or destroyed by the love of a female." This narrative structure is a companion to "the structure in which a female is rescued or destroyed by the love of a male." *The Tale of Li Wa* also has the basic structure of the story of a wandering holy aristocrat.

The Tale of Li Wa's narrative type has the story structure, "a man saved/destroyed by the love of a woman." Japanese narratives, such as *The Tale of Shintoku Maru* and *The Tale of Oguri Hangan*, also fall into this category. On the other hand, there are many versions of "a woman saved/destroyed by the love of a man," such as the stories that manifest in *Sleeping Beauty*, *Cinderella*, *White Swan*, and so on.

As is typical in *The Tale of Li Wa*, the story of a wandering holy aristocrat is also the basic type of other popular stories. The structure of the above-mentioned "man saved/destroyed by the love of a woman," and "woman saved/destroyed by the love of a man," fuse with the story of the wandering holy aristocrat to create the audience's impression.

Characters in the love story often take a four-quadrant personality type, as *The Tale of Li Wa* does, shown in Figure 5. The four quadrants' characters can be classified into four types according to their gender, status, and the social situation in which they are located, and the story is mainly composed of four persons. Speaking of Chinese examples, *Legend of the White Snake* and the inherited Peking Opera have a typical four-quadrant structure similar to *Li Wa's Tale*. There are countless examples, but I would like to mention *La Traviata* and *Swan Lake* as examples of typical romantic plays in Western Europe that follow this structure as well.

Conclusion: The Road of Love in the Eurasian Continent

Street theater is performed by the class, status, or group that does not belong to the elite class. The author or narrator often lives in a multicultural society and travels to multiple regions. The story's protagonist is discriminated against or excluded from society somehow and is directed to have universal values because of these negative circumstances. The spectators are ordinary people who cannot go to the roofed theater.

Roofed theaters would eventually replace street plays. However, the story structure created by street theater is immutable. Why does street theater adopt such a universal structure? It is likely that, when performing, directing, and watching a story in a restricted space, time, and social situation limited by the era, it is only by having the aforementioned elements that the drama can have the universality that can break this limited space, time, and hierarchy.

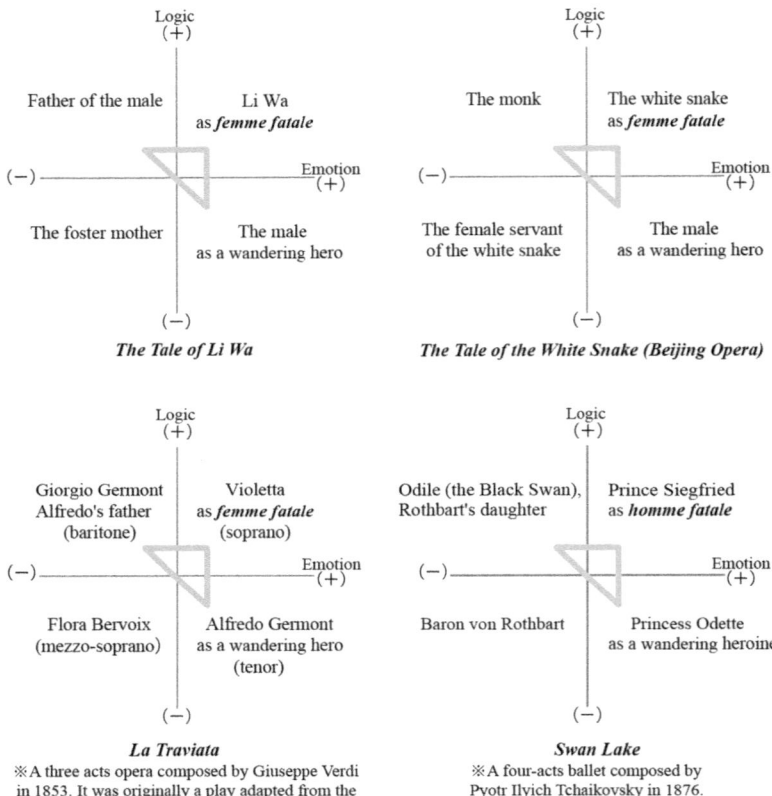

Fig.5 Four quadrant structure of love dramas

▽ triangular relationship

Lastly, I would like to summarize this article based on the type of love drama. Love is an intellectual and inner play of the individual that creates affection for the other based on rules and manners. Among the origins and spread of love stories born within cities, I position *The Tale of Li Wa* as one of the earliest love stories in eastern Eurasia. Figure 6 shows a hypothesis of the spread of the love story in Eurasia.

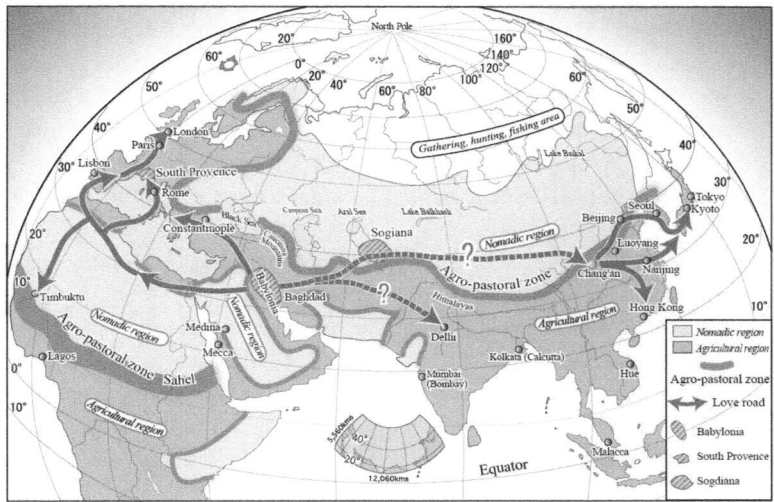

Fig.6 Spread of the love story in Eurasia

References

Campany, Robert Ford (2015): *A Garden of Marvels: Tales of Wonder from Early Medieval China*. Honolulu: University of Hawai'i Press.

Ditter, Alexei (2011): "Conceptions of Urban Space in Duan Chengshi's 'Record of Monasteries and Stupas'." *T'ang Studies* 29, pp. 62–83.

Ditter, Alexei Kamran, et al., eds. (2017): *Tales from Tang Dynasty China: Selections from the Taiping Guangji*. Indianapolis: Hackett Publishing Company.

Dudbridge, Glen (1983): *The Tale of Li Wa, Study and Critical Edition of a Chinese Story from the Ninth Century*, Oxford Monographs Series no. 4, London: Ithaca Press for the Board of the Faculty of Oriental Studies, Oxford University.

Edwards, E.D. (1938): *Chinese Prose Literature of the T'ang Period A.D.618–906*, London: Arthur Probsthain.

Feng, Linda Rui (2011a): "Negotiating Vertical Space: Walls, Vistas, and the Topographical Imagination." *T'ang Studies*, 29, pp. 27–44.

Feng, Linda Rui (2011b): "Chang'an and Narratives of Experience in Tang Tales." *Harvard Journal of Asiatic Studies*, Volume 71, Number 1, pp. 35–68.

Feng, Linda Rui (2015): *City of Marvel and Transformation, Chang'an and Narratives of Experience in Tang Dynasty China*, Honolulu: University of Hawai'I Press.

Hashimoto, Takashi (1983): "Li A den no Motif (The Motif of *The Tale of Li Wa*)," in *Obi Hakase Koki Kinen Chugoku gaku Ronshū* (Festschrift for the 70th Birthday of Professor Obi: Various issues related to Sinology), Tokyo: Kyuko Shoin, pp.471–484.

Luo, Manling (2015): *Literati Storytelling in Late Medieval China*, Seattle: University of Washington.

Mair, Victor H. (1997): *Painting and Performance: Chinese Picture Recitation and Its Indian Genesis*, Honolulu: University of Hawai'i Press.

Mair, Victor H. (1983): *Tun-huang Popular Narratives*, Cambridge: Cambridge University Press.

Nienhauser, William H. Jr. (2007): "A Third Look at " Li Wa Zhuan"," *Tang Studies* 25, pp. 91–110.

Picken, Laurence E. R. (1981-2000): *Music from the Tang Court,vol,1–vol.7*, Cambridge: Cambridge University Press.

Seo, Tatsuhiko (1987a): "The Urban Systems of Chang'an in the Sui and Tang Dynasties A.D.583-907," in M.A.J.Beg ed., *Historic Cities of Asia: An Introduction to Asian Cities from Antiquity to Pre-modern Times*, Kula Lumpur, Malaysia: Percetakan Ban Huat Seng, pp.159–200.

Seo, Tatsuhiko (1987b): " Tōdai Kōhanki no Chōan to Denki Shōsetsu : Ri A den no Bunseki o Chūshin toshite" (Late Tang Chang'an and Chuanqi tales: Focused on the Analysis of *The Tale of Li Wa*). In *Ronshū Chūgoku Shakai Seido Bunkashi no Shomondai: Hino Kaisaburō hakase shōju kinen* (Festschrift in Honor of Professor Hino Kaisaburō: Various Issues Related to Chinese Social Order and Culture), Fukuoka: Chugoku Shoten, 1987, pp. 476-505; Song Jinwen trans. in *Riben Zhongqingnian Xuezhe Lun Zhongguoshi: Liuchao Sui-Tang juan* (Essays by Young and Middle-aged Japanese Scholars on Chinese History – Six Dynasties and Sui-Tang Volume), pp. 509–553. Shanghai: Shanghai guji chubanshe, 1995; Duan Yu trans. in *Zhongguo Chengshi Shehuishi Mingbian Jingdu* (Readings of some Masterpieces of Chinese Social Urban History), Shanghai: Shanghai jiaoyu chubanshe, 2020, pp.38–75.

Seo, Tatsuhiko (2003): "Caizi" yu "Jiaren": Jiu Shiji Zhongguo de Xin de Nannǔ Renshi Xingcheng" ("Caizi" and "Jiaren": The Formation of New Gender Recognition in China in the 9th century). in Deng Xiaonan and Beijing

Daxue Zhonggu shi Yanjiu Zhongxin eds., *Tang Song Funü shi Yanjiu yu Lishi xue* (Tang-Song Women History Studies and History), Shanghai: Shanghai Cishu Chubanshe, pp. 695–722.

Seo, Tatsuhiko (2004): "The Printing Industry at the East Market in the Late Tang, "*Memoirs of the Research Department of the Toyo Bunko*, 61, pp.1–42.

Seo,Tatsuhiko (2019a): "The Tang Dynasty I", Victor Cunrui Xiong and Kenneth J. Hammond eds., *Routledge Handbook of Imperial Chinese History*, London and New York: Routledge, pp.126–143.

Seo, Tatsuhiko (2019b): "Buddhism and Commerce in Ninth-Century Chang'an: A study of Ennin's Nittō Guhō Junrei Kōki," in *Studies in Chinese Religions*, London and NewYork: Routledge, pp. 1–20.

Seo, Tatsuhiko (2019c): Gao Bingbing, Guo Xueni and Huang Haijing trans., *Sui Tang Chang'an yu Dongya Bijiao Duchengshi (The Comparative History of Tradditional Capital Cities in the Sui and Tang Dinasties)* , Xian: Xibei daxue chubanshe.

Seo,Tatsuhiko (2020): "Chōan 751 nen, Yūrashia no Henbō (Chang'an, 751: Transformation of the Eurasian Continent)," in Miura, Tōru ed., *Rekishi no Tenkanki 3: Huhen Sekai no Teiritsu(Turning Points in History 3: Trilogy of the Universal World)*, Tokyo: Yamakawa Shuppansha, pp.182-228.

Shields, Anna (2014): "Gossip, Anecdote, and Literary History: Representations of the Yuanhe Era in Tang Anecdote Collections." in *Idle Talk: Gossip and Anecdote in Traditional China*, Berkeley: University of California Press, pp. 107–131.

Tang, Keyang (2010): "The Ward Walls and Gates of Tang Chang'an as Seen in 'The Tale of Li Wa.'" in Roger Des Forges et al. eds., *Chinese Walls in Time and Space: A Multidisciplinary Perspective*, Ithaca, New York: Cornell University East Asia Program, pp.113–138.

Tsai, S-C Kevin (2004): "Ritual and Gender in the ‚Tale of Li Wa'," *Chinese Literature: Essays, Articles, Reviews (CLEAR)* 26, pp. 99–127.

The Semi-Circular Theatre in Seleucid and Arsacid Babylon[1]

MITSUMA Yasuyuki

In 53 BC, General Surena of the Arsacid dynasty of Parthia defeated the Roman army near Carrhae (ancient Harran) in Upper Mesopotamia, killing its commander Crassus, one of the First Triumvirate. Crassus's head was sent to King Urōd (Hyrodes or Orodes) II of the Arsacids, who was hosting King Artavasdes II of Armenia. Plutarch's *Vitae Parallelae* (Plut. Vit. Crass. 33) describes the event in which Crassus's head was brought to Armenia (Perrin 1916: 421–423). The scene shows that Greek tragedies were often performed in Armenian and Arsacid courts. When the head was brought to the king's banquet, a tragic actor called Jason was singing a part of the *Bacchae* of Euripides. Then Sillaces arrived at the banquet hall and cast the head into the hall. Jason seized the head, acting the role of Agave, sang as follows (Perrin 1916: 421):

'We bring from the mountain
A tendril fresh-cut to the palace,
A wonderful prey.'

---

[1] The research for this chapter is funded by JSPS KAKENHI Grants JP17H04527, JP18H05445, and JP18K00987. I thank the Trustees of the British Museum for allowing me to study the original cuneiform tablets cited in this chapter. I also thank Misa Hiyama (University of Tokyo) and Editage (www.editage.com) for English language editing.

The abbreviations in this chapter follow the lists in OCD[4] and in Streck (2016–2018) except those listed in the abbreviation list at the end of the chapter. Lines on cuneiform tablets of Babylonian Astronomical Diaries and Babylonian Chronicles are cited according to the method used in ADART 1: 38. The format 'n/n-1 BC' shows the Julian equivalent to a year in the Babylonian calendar, if unspecified. Since a Babylonian year begins in spring, the beginning and the end of the year should be dated to different years in the Julian calendar. Roman numerals are used to refer to Babylonian months.

The chorus made a dialogue with Agave, as follows (Perrin 1916: 423):

(*Chorus*) 'Who slew him?'
(*Agave*) 'Mine is the honour,'

This delighted everyone. In the context of the tragedy, there was a display of unusual enthusiasm regarding a strange object—Crassus's head—as if it were a prop in the play.

In this occurrence, a feast venue was used as the stage for such a tragedy, but semi-circular theatres, such as those built in the Hellenistic and Roman world, were used for full-scale performances. Such semi-circular theatres also existed in Babylon, the old central city of Babylonia (modern southern Iraq). The theatre existed when the Seleucid (Macedonian) and the Arsacid dynasties ruled Babylon (305/304–141/140 BC and 141/140 BC–AD 224) and functioned as a meeting place for the Greco-Macedonian resident group called the 'citizens of Babylon' (*puliṭānu/puliṭê ša ina Bābili* in Akkadian, the traditional language of ancient Babylonia). This group is differentiated from the traditional resident group of Babylon called 'Babylonians' (people who call themselves *Bābilāya* in Akkadian). The Akkadian term for 'citizens' was derived from the Greek word πολῖται ('citizens'). The official who represented the 'citizens of Babylon' was called the 'governor of Babylon' (*paḫāt Bābili*). Furthermore, it is highly probable that the 'citizens' had an institution called the '(council of) elders' (πελιγᾶνες in Greek; *peliganānu* in Akkadian), which also existed in cities such as Seleucia on the Tigris and Laodicea by the Sea (Mitsuma 2019: 298–299, 303–304).

The 'citizens' were introduced to Babylon during the reign of Antiochus III (222/221–187/186 BC),[2] or that of Antiochus IV (175/174–164/163 BC)[3] of the Seleucids. Since the reign of Antiochus IV, or more precisely from 172/171 BC, they were often mentioned in Akkadian cuneiform records such as the Babylonian Astronomical Diaries and Babylonian Chronicles.[4] The scholars that compiled those records were employed by Esagil, the temple of Marduk in Babylon, which was the centre of 'Babylonians' (Mitsuma 2017: 42–43). The

---

2   Boiy 2004: 207–208.
3   Van der Spek 2005: 396; van der Spek 2009: 107–108.
4   For the attestations, see Mitsuma 2019: 295–296; Datable diaries are published in ADART 1–3, and Babylonian Chronicles after Alexander the Great are to be published in BCHP.

introduction of the 'citizens' into Babylon by Antiochus (III/IV) is recorded in the chronicle BCHP 14 (dated to 163/162 BC).[5]

BCHP 14 Obv.'
Transliteration
2 ˡᵘ́Ia-'-man-na-a-a-ni MU-šú-nu ˡᵘ́p[u-li-ṭa-nu]
3 šá ina IGI-ma ina qí-bi šá ᵐAn LUGAL ina E[ᵏⁱ KU₄ᵐᵉˢ̌]
4 u Ì.GIŠ ŠÉŠᵐᵉˢ̌ I[ì]b-bu-ú ˡᵘ́pu-I[i-ṭa-nu]
5 šá ina ᵘʳᵘSi-Iu-ki-'-'a-a URU LUGAL-ú-t[u]
6 šá ina muḫ-ḫi ⁱᵈIDIGNA u ÍD LUGAL

Translation
2 the Greeks (or Ionians), who are called 'citi[zens'],
3 who formerly [entered] Babylon by the order of King An(tiocus),
4 and smear themselves with oil like the citi[zens]
5 of Seleucia, the city of kingship,
6 which is on the Tigris and the King's Canal

The chronicle BCHP 14 clearly states that the 'citizens' were 'Greeks', or more precisely, 'Ionians' (people from the Aegean area, including Greece and western Anatolia; see Rollinger 2009: 32, 38; Yamada 2019: 221–222). Although the group of 'citizens' may have included people from Greece and western Anatolia, the group also included those from other regions who adopted Greek lifestyle and customs. Greek citizens' habits included 'smearing themselves with oil'; they smeared olive oil over their bodies while exercising naked in gymnasiums or training schools (van der Spek 2005: 396; van der Spek 2009: 108). Being accepted by a gymnasium was a sign of citizenship (van der Spek 2005: 396; van der Spek 2009: 108), and the existence of a gymnasium in Babylon is evident from the Greek inscription SEG 7 39[6] that records the winners of games in 111/110 BC of the Babylonian calendar[7], or in the first half of 111/110

---

5   The text of BCHP 14 with the restored signs is published in van der Spek 2005: 403–404. Mitsuma 2019: 296–297 cites the text of Obv.' 1–7 with some changes in the way of transliteration and shows a new translation of the part. The following transliteration bases on the text citation of Mitsuma 2019: 296, but the translation changes in some points.
6   Van der Spek 2005: 398; van der Spek 2009: 110. For the text of SEG 7 39, see van der Spek 2005: 406–407.
7   Van der Spek 2005: 398; van der Spek 2009: 110.

BC[8], and attests the existence of the office of the training manager of a gymnasium, or the gymnasiarch (unfortunately, his personal name is damaged and unclear).

The semi-circular theatre in Babylon served as a meeting place for the 'citizens (of Babylon)', and letters were often read aloud in this theatre in the early Arsacid period addressing the 'citizens' and their representative, the 'governor of Babylon' (van der Spek 2001: 455; Sciandra 2012: 236). The ruins of the theatre were uncovered in 1904 by the excavators of Babylon under the command of Robert Koldewey (Mallwitz 1994: 3; Potts 2011: 240).

According to Potts (2011: 240–243), the theatre was built and rebuilt in two phases, the first of which can be divided into three sub-phases. The theatre of Phase I was built in the period following the entrance of Alexander the Great into Babylon (331/330 BC) (van der Spek 2001: 446). A horizontal stage building (skene) was constructed that had three doorways that opened to the orchestra in front (the place where the chorus and actors performed, 21.8m in diameter). In addition, passages (parodoi) to the orchestra were constructed between the skene and the surrounding seating area (koilon). The parodoi were limited by the arc of the koilon; that is, when viewed from the skene, the opposite side of the passages became farther as one moved inside (see Mallwitz 1994: plate 8; Potts 2011: 241: figure 1). The theatre was thought to be renovated after the 'citizens' were introduced in Babylon (Phase I_2, for the date of the renovation, see Mallwitz 1994: 20; van der Spek 2001: 445–446). In this phase, a proscenium was expanded in front of the skene; actors also performed there (see Mallwitz 1994: plate 8; Potts 2011: 242: figure 2). In Phase I_3, the orchestra was expanded to 22.16m in diameter (see Mallwitz 1994: plate 9; Potts 2011: 242: figure 3). The theatre of Phase I_3 seems to have functioned until the beginning of the first century BC because it is mentioned in the Astronomical Diaries (as É IGI.DU$_8$.A, *bīt tāmarti*[9]) several times during 162/161–83/82 BC (van der Spek 2001: 448–455). The Phase I_3 theatre was destroyed or fell out of use since then (the destruction's *terminus post quem* seems to be 83/82 BC, see Potts 2011: 248), and the Phase II theatre was rebuilt in the first or second century AD (Mallwitz 1994: 20–21; van der Spek 2001: 446; Potts 2011: 248).

---

8   The two year numbers show the Julian equivalent to the Macedonian year, which begins in the autumn of 111 BC and ends in the autumn of 110 BC. For the dating of the inscription, see Assar 2003: 177.

9   This Akkadian expression seems to be an equivalent to the Greek word θέατρον, 'theatre' (see van der Spek 2001: 447).

This theatre seems to have been reconstructed in a Roman rather than a Greek style, and a palaestra (wrestling school) was added to the theatre (see Mallwitz 1994: plate 11a; Potts 2011: 242–243; 243: figure 4).

One can see how this theatre was used in several passages in the Astronomical Diaries. It likely hosted plays, but all the accounts concerning the theatre from the diaries of the Arsacid period describe letters read aloud there (ADART 3 -140A 'Rev. 5'–6'; -132D$_2$ 'Rev.' 14'–22'; -124B 'Rev.' 17'–19'; -118A 'Rev. 18'–21'; -87C 'Rev. 30'; and also -82B 'Obv.' 21' seems to show that something was read aloud in the theatre). According to ADART 3 -140A 'Rev. 5'–6', -132D$_2$ 'Rev.' 14'–22'; -124B 'Rev.' 17'–19', and -118A 'Rev. 18'–21', the letters were addressed to the 'governor of Babylon' and the 'citizens of Babylon'. According to ADART 3 -124B 'Rev.' 17'–19', a letter of the king Artabān I of the Arsacids was carried by the king's messenger and read aloud in the theatre in X.125/124 BC. In ADART 3 -118A 'Rev. 18'–21', it is clearly stated that the letter read aloud in VII.119/118 BC was the 'parchment document of King Aršak' and was certainly sent by Mihrdāt II, the Arsacid king who ruled Babylon at the time. The following are the accounts of the two letters read aloud in the theatre, transliterated and translated. Copies of the cuneiform texts are shown in Figures 1–2 at the end of this chapter.

ADART 3 -124B (BM 45693 + 45853) 'Rev.'
Transliteration
17' [x x x] ^{lú}KIN.GI$_4$.A LUGAL šá ^{kuš}SAR^{meš} na-šu-ú ana E^{ki} KU$_4$-ub U$_4$ BI ^{kuš}SAR^m[^{eš} LUGA]L šá ana muḫ-ḫi ^{lú}pa-ḫat E^{ki} u ^{lú}pu-li-te-e šá ina E^{ki} SAR^{meš} ina É IGI.DU$_8$.A šá-su-ú um-ma ṣal-tu$_4$
18' [KI ^{m}] ˹Pi-it-˺ti-˹it˺ ^{lú}KÚR NIM.MA^{ki} DÙ-ma 15-lim ERÍN-ni MÈ ina ŠÀ ERÍN-ni-šú ina ^{giš}TU[KUL ú-šám-]qit-ma^{10} ḫa-as-ru-ú^{11} ina lìb-bi ERÍN-ni-iá NU GAR-an ^{kur}NIM.MA^{ki} pa-aṭ gim-ri-šú ina ^{giš}TUKUL SÌG-aṣ ^{m}Pi-it-ti-it
19' [x] ˹x x x KI˺$^{?12}$ aṣ-bat U$_4$ BI (omitted)

---

10   The restoration ^{giš}TU[KUL ú-šám-] is shown in van der Spek 2001: 452.
11   The sign aṣ was not transliterated in preceding editions (ADART 3: 278; Del Monte 1997: 142; van der Spek 2001: 452; Haubold 2019: 287; Visscher 2019: 259). The word ḫasrū is the stative 3m. plural of ḫasāru. The verb is used to show a break of cuneiform text in the scribal remark at BBR 43 8'–9' (CAD, s.v. "ḫesēru"). Here, the word ḫasrū seems to be used to show the part had been 'broken' in the source text of -124B. Judging from the context, one or two words are lost.
12   The restoration [^{lú}]KÚR NIM.MA^{ki} is expected here, but the remaining sign traces do not necessarily support this restoration.

Translation

17' [....] A messenger of the king who carried parchment document entered Babylon. On the same day, the parchment document of the [king], which was written to the governor of Babylon and the citizens of Babylon, was read aloud in the theatre as follows: A battle

18' I made [with] Pittit, the Elamite enemy, and [I put] 15,000 battle troops among his army to the [weapon], and—broken—did not occur in my army. Striking all over Elam with the weapon, Pittit,

19' [....] ...., I seized. On the same day, (omitted)

ADART 3 -118A (BM 41693) 'Rev.
Transliteration

18' (omitted) [ITI] BI U_4 15.KAM ^{kuš}SAR^{meš} šá ^{m}Ar-šá-ka-a LU[GAL šá ana UGU]

19' ⸢lú⸣pa-ḫat`E^{ki} u ^{lú}pu-li-ṭa-an šá ina E^{ki} SAR^{meš} ina É IGI.DU$_8$.A šá-su-ú ak-ka-i šá[13] ^{lú}ERÍN^{meš} MAḪ^{meš} NIGIN-ma ù ana LÚ.NE GIN^{meš} ana UGU DUMU LUGAL u ^{lú}ERÍN^{meš}-šú šá URU^{meš} S[UD^{meš}][14]

20' [šá ^{kur}G]u$^?$-ti-i[15] šá a-na ^{m}Ár-ta-ba-na-a ŠEŠ-iá GAZ-ku ù as-di-ir ana tar-ṣi-šú-nu u LÚ.NE e-pu-šú[16] it-ti-šú-nu GAZ-tu$_4$ GAL-tu$_4$ ina lìb-bi-šú-nu áš-kun e-lat 2 LÚ ⸢x⸣ [....]

21' [x x x] ul GAZ^{meš} u DUMU LUGAL u ERÍN^{meš}-šú TA LÚ.NE BAL-ma a-na ár-ki-šú a-na KUR^{meš} dan-nu-tú iḫ-ḫi-is ITI BI (omitted)

Translation

18' (omitted) On the 15th of the same [month], parchment document of King
Aršak[, which]

19' was written [to] the governor of Babylon and the citizens of Babylon, was read
aloud in the theatre as follows: A large army gathered and went to the battle against the prince and his army of the re[mote] cities

20' [of Gu]ti, who killed Artabān, my brother. And I arranged a battle line against

---

13   For *akkā'i ša* as a direct speech marker, see Sciandra 2012: 235n37.
14   The restoration is shown in van der Spek 2001: 453.
15   The restoration is shown in van der Spek 2001: 453.
16   The last sign šú only represents the vowel /š/ (See Hyatt 1941: 23, 56).

them, fought with them, and committed a great massacre among them. Except
for two [....]
21' [....] they were not killed[17] and the prince and his army withdrew from the
battle and retreated to the rear, to the difficult mountains. In the same month,
(omitted)

These two documents describe the victory of the Arsacid kings (Artabān I and his son Mihrdāt II, both of whom are called the Arsacid coronation name 'Aršak' in contemporary sources) against two different enemies, one is 'Pittit (Pitthides), the Elamite enemy', while the other is called 'the prince and his army of the re[mote] cities [of Gu]ti'. As Haruta (1998, 183–184) points out, the Elymaean leader Pittit can be identified as Pitthides, whose eyes were gouged out and whom the envoys sent to King Arsaces (Aršak) from Seleucia (on the Tigris) were forced to face as a warning (Diod. Sic. 34/35:19). The Akkadian name 'Guti' is an archaic appellation for the regions in the northeast direction from Babylonia (Zadok 1985: 143–144), and in this case, it is used to refer to the territory of the steppe nomads in Central Asia (Haruta 1998: 186). The nomads (Scythians) revenged by Mihrdāt II are also mentioned in Justin's epitome of Pompey Trogue's *Historiae Philippicae* (Just. *Epit.* 42:2:1–5). Justin describes Mihrdāt II's wars against Scythians as a whole in Justin (*Epit.* 42:2:5), but the diary ADART 3 -118A 'Rev. 18'–21' seems to describe a part of the wars. Justin describes the death of Mihrdāt II's father, King Artabān I, caused by a wound in the battle with Tocharii, a group of Scythians,[18] in Justin (*Epit.* 42:2:2); on the other hand, Mihrdāt II's letter quoted in the diary ADART 3 - 118A considers the murder of prince Artabān ($^{m}Ár$-ta-ba-na-a), brother of King Aršak (Mihrdāt II), as the direct cause of the battle against nomad troops led by a prince (could be identified as Tocharii). In short, Justin (*Epit.* 42:2:2) may have mistaken prince Artabān for King Artabān I (Mitsuma 2012: 341) because he makes a similar mistake in an adjacent chapter (Just. *Epit.* 42:4:1), in which he confuses Mihrdāt III with Mihrdāt II.

---

17   The sentence 'Except for two [....] they were not killed' probably describes the exceptionally minimal damage to the 'large army' of the King Aršak (Mihrdāt II) mentioned in Line 19'.
18   Strabo (11:8:2) mentions Τόχαροι as a part of nomadic Scythians.

Comparing these two victory reports passed on to Babylon, we find the following common features. They may represent the character of the royal propaganda of the Arsacids.[19]

1. Both argue victory over a large number of enemies ('[put] 15,000 battle troops among his army to the [weapon]' and 'committed a great massacre among them').
2. Both deny the occurrence of something negative in the Arsacid army ('—broken—did not occur in my army' and 'Except for two [....] they were not killed'; The subject of the former is lost, but the context suggests that it is a negative thing for the Arsacids).
3. Both claim that they widely overwhelmed their opponent's land ('striking all over Elam with the weapon' and 'the prince and his army withdrew from the battle and retreated to the rear, to the difficult mountains').

Regarding the victory over Elymais (Elam), the diary ADART 3 -124B quotes another letter just before the quotation of the letter sent by King Artabān I. This letter was written by Aspasinē—the king of Mesene, a small kingdom located in the Persian Gulf—to the 'general of Babylonia', the commander of the Arsacid troops stationed in the province Babylonia,[20] and read aloud to the 'citizens of Babylon' on 2.X.125/124 BC. Regarding the arrival of the Artabān's letter, its date is unclear because the tablet is damaged, but it should be dated later in X.125/124 BC, because the event is recorded in some lines after the arrival and reading out of the Aspasinē's letter in the historical part of X.125/124 BC of the diary ADART 3 -124B. The following is the transliteration and translation of the Akkadian text concerning the letter or the parchment document of Aspasinē. A copy of the cuneiform text is shown in Figure 1.

ADART 3 -124B 'Rev.'
Transliteration
12' (omitted) ITI BI U₄ 2.KAM ⸢x⸣ [x ᵏᵘ]ˢSAR^(meš) šá ᵐAs-pa-a-si-né-e LUGAL A^(meš)-šá-nu-ú[21] šá ana muḫ-ḫi ^(lú)GAL ERÍN-ni KUR URI^(ki) iš-ṭur it-taḫ-ḫi

---

19   Sciandra (2012: 234–236) discusses the outline of propagandistic letters of the Arsacids cited in the Astronomical Diaries.
20   For the function of the office, see Mitsuma 2002: 39, 43, 46; Mitsuma 2009: 155.
21   A^(meš)-šá-nu-ú could be read mê-šanû and seems to be a corrupt form of mû-šanûtu 'other warters' (Del Monte 1997: 117). It could reflect the regional name of Mesene (Mēšān in

13' [ina DA ˡᵘpu-li-]te-e²² šá ina Eᵏⁱ šá-su-ú um-ma ina ITI BI U₄ 15.KAM ᵐAr-šá-kam LUGAL u ᵐPi-i[t-ti-i̯]t ˡᵘKÚR NIM.MAᵏⁱ ṣal-tu₄ KI a-ḫa-meš DÙ-u' LUGAL BAD₅.BAD₅ ˡᵘERÍN-ni ᵏᵘʳNIM.MAᵏⁱ ina ᵍⁱˢTUKUL GAR-ʾan⌉ ᵐPi-it-ti-it

14' [ˡᵘKÚR NIM.MAᵏⁱ]²³ iṣ-bat ITI BI (omitted)

Translation

12' (omitted) On the 2nd of the same month, …. parchment document of Aspasinē,

the king of Mesene, which he had written to the general of Babylonia, arrived (and)

13' was read aloud [next to the citi]zens of Babylon, as follows: On the 15th of this

month (of the previous month?), King Aršak and Pittit, the Elamite

enemy, fought with each other. The king used the weapon to defeat the Elamite

army. Pittit,

14' [the Elamite enemy,] he seized. In the same month, (omitted)

This letter conveys the Arsacid victory over Elymais in a subdued tone. It reports only the facts that King Aršak (Artabān I) and Pittit battled and the former defeated and seized the latter. The simplicity of this report suggests that Artabān I's letter, which is quoted after this statement, contains considerable exaggerations. News of the victory, which was brilliantly conveyed in the semi-circular theatre, should have been received sceptically, at least by the scholar who wrote the diary ADART 3 -124B and quoted Aspasinē's and Artabān's letters side by side (who was not a member of the 'citizens of Babylon' but one of the 'Babylonians'). However, the 'citizens of Babylon', who heard the victory report of Artabān I in the theatre, might have, at least officially, showed great enthusiasm for the propagandistic news, although they had already known of Artabān's victory from the letter of Aspasinē. Aspasinē's letter may itself point to a connection between the 'citizens of Babylon' and a potential adversary of the Arsacids. King Aspasinē's Mesene was a power

---

Middle Persian, see Hansman 1992) and refer to the region situated on the waters of the Persian Gulf.

22 This restoration is shown in van der Spek 2001: 451.
23 This restoration is shown in van der Spek 2001: 452.

that temporarily occupied Babylon in 127/126 BC (Del Monte 1997: 249),[24] and while it lost control of Babylon at the time, it maintained contact with neighbouring Babylonia and thus conveyed the information of Artabān's victory to the military commander of the Arsacid troops in the province, the 'general of Babylonia'. Mesene's concern regarding Babylonia is also attested in the diary ADART 3 -124B 'Obv.' 5'–6'. According to the historical account of VIII.125/124 BC, Aspasinē's son, Timotheus, went out from Babylon to visit the 'general of Babylonia' in Seleucia on the Tigris, the Arsacid political centre of Babylonia. A son of Aspasinē was arrested (probably in Seleucia) and sent back to his father in the following month IX (ADART 3 -124B 'Obv.' 19'–20', unfortunately, the name of the arrestee is severely damaged in Line 19'). The letter from Aspasinē about the victory of Artabān I against Pittit arrived at Babylon on 2.X.125/124 BC. Presumably, if Artabān had failed at Elymais, King Aspasinē, the 'general of Babylonia', and even the 'citizens of Babylon', might have launched a resistance movement against Artabān I. King Aspasinē's letter may have been a message to the general and the 'citizens' that the situation no longer allowed such resistance. The event recorded on ADART 3 -124B 'Rev.' 14'–16' may show the reaction of the 'citizens' to this message (see the text of van der Spek 2001: 452). On 15.X.125/124BC, they took away the θρόνος ('throne' in Greek), which King Aspasinē had dedicated to the god Marduk during his occupation of Babylon, from the treasury attached to the 'Day-One Temple'.[25] This event shows the diminished authority of Aspasinē in Babylon. The 'citizens' might have further shown (even if they were merely pretending) pro-Arsacid sentiments toward the propagandistic victory report of Artabān, which was read aloud later in the theatre (which is recorded just after the sacrilege on ADART 3 -124B 'Rev.' 17'–19'), being afraid of a purge of Artabān's potential adversaries. We may understand the warning introduction of Pittit by King Arsaces to the envoys of Seleucia on the Tigris, who were sent to beg his pardon for Seleuceans' torture of his general, Enius (Diod. Sic. 34/35:19), as a threat against a hostile group, made after the Arsacid victory over Elymais (see also Haruta 1998: 183–184).

The reading of a letter in the semi-circular theatre reflects a deep political situation in which the ulterior motives of each power collided and became intertwined.

---

24   Aspasinē might have occupied Babylon from 128/127 to 127/126 BC (Mitsuma 2009: 168).

25   For the 'Day-One Temple' and its treasury, see Mitsuma 2008: 98.

Abbreviations

ADART	Sachs, Abraham J./Hunger, Hermann (1988–2014): Astronomical Diaries and Related Texts from Babylonia, vols. 1–3, 5–7, Vienna: VÖAW.
BCHP	van der Spek, Robartus J./Finkel, Irving L./Pirngruber, Reinhard/Stevens, Kathryn (eds.) (forthcoming): Babylonian Chronographic Texts from the Hellenistic Period, Atlanta: SBL (Finkel, Irving L./van der Spek, Robartus J．). [n.d.]: Babylonian Chronicles of the Hellenistic Period, scholarly edition, accessed 19 August 2016 at Livius.org. http://www.livius.org/sources/about/mesopotamian-chronicles/).
OCD[4]	Hornblower, Simon/Spawforth, Antony/Eidinow, Esther (eds.) (2012): The Oxford Classical Dictionary, fourth edition, Oxford: Oxford University Press.

References

Assar, Gholamreza F. (2003): "Parthian Calendars at Babylon and Seleucia on the Tigris." In: Iran 41: pp. 171–191.

Boiy, Tom (2004): Late Achaemenid and Hellenistic Babylon, Louvain: Peeters.

Del Monte, Giuseppe F. (1997): Testi dalla Babilonia ellenistica, vol. 1, Testi cronografici, Pisa: Istituti editoriali e poligrafici internazionali.

Hansman, John (1992): "CHARACENE and CHARAX." In: Yarshater, Ehsan (ed.), Encyclopaedia iranica, vol. 5, Costa Mesa, CA: Mazda, pp. 363–365.

Haruta, Seiro (1998): "A Primary Source for the History of the Arshakid Parthia: Astronomical Diaries from 164 B.C. to 61 B.C." In: Bulletin of the Society for Near Eastern Studies in Japan 41/2: pp. 181–193 (in Japanese).

Haubold, Johannes (2019): "History and Historiography in the Early Parthian Diaries." In: Haubold, Johannes, et al. (eds.), Keeping Watch in Babylon: The Astronomical Diaries in Context, Leiden: Brill, pp. 269–293.

Hyatt, James P. (1941): The Treatment of Final Vowels in Early Neo-Babylonian, New Haven, CT: Yale University Press.

Mallwitz, Alfred (1994): "Das Theater von Babylon." In: Wetzel, Friedrich, et al., Das Babylon der Spätzeit, second edition, Berlin: Mann, pp. 3–22.

Mitsuma, Yasuyuki (2002): "Offices of Generals in Seleucid and Aršakid Babylonia." Bulletin of the Society for Near Eastern Studies in Japan 45/2, pp. 26–55 (in Japanese).

Mitsuma, Yasuyuki (2008): "Ištar of Babylon in "Day-One Temple"." In: Nouvelles Assyriologiques Brèves et Utilitaires 2008, pp. 96–99.

Mitsuma, Yasuyuki (2009): "Royal Officials and the City of Babylon in the Seleucid and Arsacid Periods: A Study of "Diaries"." PhD Dissertation, University of Tokyo (in Japanese).

Mitsuma, Yasuyuki (2012): "Sufferings of the Arsacids." In: The Historical Science Society of Japan (ed.), Sources of World History, vol. 1, Tokyo: Iwanami, pp. 340–341 (in Japanese).

Mitsuma, Yasuyuki (2017): "The Relationship Between the Cuneiform Akkadian Texts, "Late Babylonian Chronicles" and "Babylonian Astronomical Diaries"." In: Journal of Historical Studies 964, pp. 35–45 (in Japanese).

Mitsuma, Yasuyuki (2019): "The Relationship Between Greco-Macedonian Citizens and the "Council of Elders" in the Arsacid Period: New Evidence from Astronomical Diary BM 35269 + 35347 + 35358." In: Haubold, Johannes, et al. (eds.), Keeping Watch in Babylon: The Astronomical Diaries in Context, Leiden: Brill, pp. 294–306.

Perrin, Bernadotte (trans.) (1916): Plutarch's Lives with an English Translation, vol. 3, London: Heinemann.

Potts, Daniel. T. (2011): "The *politai* and the *bīt tāmartu*: The Seleucid and Parthian Theatres of the Greek Citizens of Babylon." In: Cancik-Kirschbaum, Eva, et al. (eds.), Babylon: Wissenskultur in Orient und Okzident, Berlin: De Gruyter, pp. 239–251.

Rollinger, Robert (2009): "Near Eastern Perspectives on the Greeks." In: Boys-Stones, Geroge, et al. (eds.), The Oxford Handbook of Hellenic Studies, Oxford: Oxford University Press, pp. 32–47.

Sciandra, Roberto (2012): "The Babylonian Correspondence of the Seleucid and Arsacid Dynasties: New Insights into the Relations Between Court and City during the Late Babylonian Period." In: Wilhelm, Gernot (ed.), Organization, Representation, and Symbols of Power in the Ancient Near East: Proceedings of the 54th Rencontre Assyriologique Internationale at Würzburg 20–25 July 2008, Winona Lake, IN: Eisenbrauns, pp. 225–248.

Streck, Michael P. (ed.) (2016–2018): Reallexikon der Assyriologie und vorderasiatischen Archäologie, vol. 15, Waschung. A – Zypresse, Ausgewählte Nachträge, Index, Berlin: De Gruyter.

van der Spek, Robartus J. (2001): "The Theatre of Babylon in Cuneiform." In: van Soldt, Wilfred H. (ed.), Veenhof Anniversary Volume: Studies Presented to Klaas R. Veenhof on the Occasion of His Sixty-fifth Birthday, Leiden: Nederlands Instituut voor het Nabije Oosten, pp. 445–456.

van der Spek, Robartus J. (2005): "Ethnic Segregation in Hellenistic Babylon," In: van Soldt, Wilfred H. (ed.), Ethnicity in Ancient Mesopotamia: Papers Read at the 48th Rencontre Assyriologique Internationale, Leiden 1–4 July 2002, Leiden: Nederlands Instituut voor het Nabije Oosten, pp. 393–408.

van der Spek, Robartus J. (2009): "Multi-ethnicity and Ethnic Segregation in Hellenistic Babylon." In: Derks, Ton/Roymans, Nico (eds.), Ethnic Constructs in Antiquity: The Role of Power and Tradition, Amsterdam: Amsterdam University Press, pp. 101–115.

Visscher, Marijn (2019): "Royal Presence in the Astronomical Diaries." In: Haubold, Johannes, et al. (eds.), Keeping Watch in Babylon: The Astronomical Diaries in Context, Leiden: Brill, pp. 237–268.

Yamada, Shigeo (2019): "Neo-Assyrian Trading Posts on the East Mediterranean Coast and "Ionians": An Aspect of Assyro–Greek Contact." In: Nakata, Ichiro, et al. (eds.), Prince of the Orient: Ancient Near Eastern Studies in Memory of H. I. H. Prince Takahito Mikasa, Tokyo: The Society for Near Eastern Studies in Japan, pp. 221–235.

Zadok, Ran (1985): *Geographical Names According to New- and Late-Babylonian Texts*, Wiesbaden: Reichert.

Figures

Fig. 1: Copy of ADART 3 -124B (BM 45693 + 45853) 'Rev.' 12'–14', 17'–19' (part, tracing of the photograph by the author, taken with courtesy of the Trustees of the British Museum)

Fig. 2: Copy of ADART 3 -118A (BM 41693) 'Rev. 18'–21' (part, tracing of the photograph by the author, taken with courtesy of the Trustees of the British Museum)

The Perspectival Stage in Sebastiano Serlio's *Second Book of Architecture* (1545) and its German Reception in the Context of *Wohlstand*

Hans Joachim DETHLEFS

1. Introduction: The Simultaneous Experience of Space and Time

The present study examines the perceptions of space and time ushered in by the re-interpretation of the *teatro all'antica* in the Italian Renaissance. The designation *all'antica* refers to early modern architects and architectural theorists' attempts at archaeological reconstruction, drawing on the fifth book of Vitruvius's theory of architecture, which deals with the Roman theatre. The focus of this investigation will be on the *Second Book of Architecture* (1545) by the Italian Sebastiano Serlio (1475–1554) and its reception in the German-speaking world of the sixteenth century in the two architectural books (1547/1548) by Walter Hermann Ryff (ca. 1500–1548).

The line of inquiry developed here with respect to the perception of space and time in the Renaissance theatre draws on the findings of the Austrian art historian Dagobert Frey. In his work "Audience and Stage", published in 1946, Frey writes of a fundamental shift in perception in the transition from the late Gothic period to the Renaissance. The new perspectival stage, he argues, led to a "simultaneous experience of space and time for which everything that is present is also regarded and presented as such" (Frey 1946: 180).[1] In this understanding, the spectator's gaze no longer follows shifting action as the players flit between adjacent flat or bay-like *mansiones* on a divided stage [fig. 1: Terences: Comoediae, Strasbourg 1496]. The perspectival stage of the Renaissance reduces these sites to single staggered spatial images. The spectator's

---

1 Cf. also Jacquot 1964: 474–83; Molinari 1964: 61–72.

gaze thus travels from front to back; its direction remains unchanged. Three aspects will be analyzed in closer detail then: first, the perception of temporal structure enabled by the introduction of staggered stage sets offering a central perspective; second, the specific spatial perception with respect to an enclosed, roofed interior conceived in analogy to the public town square; and third, the combination of the spatial and temporal dimensions regarding how they shaped the experience of the contemporary audience.

2. Harmony Realized at a Single Glance – "in un' solo sguardo"

When Serlio's *Trattato sopra le Scene* was published in his *Second Book of Architecture*, the first codification of a geometrically constructed linear perspective centered on a single vanishing point was already over a hundred years old. Following Leon Battista Alberti's (1404–1472) *De Pictura* of 1435/1436, Leonardo da Vinci (1452–1519) continued the development of perspective in painting: the soft transitions in skies, creating gradual spatial depth, increase the complexity of perspectival depictions. Leonardo praises the superior potential of perspective in painting; in an early proposition of ca. 1490–92, he lauds the painter as "Signore d'ogni sorte di gente e di tutte le cose" – "master of all people and all things": he is able to depict everything in the universe ("ch'è nell universo per essentia") in well-proportioned harmony ("una proportionata armonia"), at a single glance – "in un' solo sguardo" (Vinci 1882: I, 18 (§13). The introductory passage of Serlio's treatise on the theatre reads like he is paraphrasing Leonardo's hymn to the all-embracing technique of perspective. However, Serlio limits the depicted space of stage perspective to depictions of urban squares and roads.

> Here the art of perspective gives us in a little space a view of superb palaces, vast temples, and houses of all kinds, and, both near and far, spacious squares, surrounded by various ornate buildings. There are long vistas of avenues with intersecting streets, triumphal arches, soaring columns, pyramids, obelisques, and a thousand other marvels, all enriched by innumerable lights (large, medium, small according to their position), at times so

skillfully placed that they seem like so many sparkling jewels – diamonds, rubies, sapphires, emeralds, and other gems (Serlio 1545: 64).[2]

Serlio mentions Leonardo in his second book: he was clearly acquainted with his studies on perspective (Serlio 1545: 39).[3] Leonardo's proposition is part of the *paragone* debate, the rivals' dispute on how to rank the fine arts. The competition between the media of the word and the image drives Leonardo's self-reflection: poets can only show beauty bit by bit ("à parte à parte"), argues his *Che differentia è dalla pittura alla poesia* of ca. 1490–92, "always re-concealing the parts it has just shown"; but if beauty is divided up and "pronounced in separate temporal sections, the memory does not receive any harmony ('non riceve alcuna armonia')" (Vinci 1882: I, 38-9 (§ 21). Leonardo's verdict on the inferiority of verbal description is not intended to denigrate the theatre: on one page of the *Codex Atlanticus* of ca. 1485–1495, he sketches a stage with spatial depth with two tapering facades, one of the earliest visualizations of a perspectival stage in the early modern period [fig. 2a/b: Leonardo da Vinci, stage setting, Windsor 12,461 and 12,720, ca. 1485-95]. The sketch anticipates Serlio's system (Flechsig 1894: 76–83; Schöne 1933: 11–13; Kindermann 1959: 97–98; Brauneck 1993: I, 462–65; Kotte 2013: 192; Johnson 2018: 60–67).[4]

Serlio emphatically welcomes the adaption of perspectival painting for the stage: for him, few things bring "greater contentment to the eye and satisfaction to the spirit ('animo') than the unveiling to our view of a stage setting ('apparato di una scena')" (Serlio 1545: 64 = Hewitt 1958: 24). His theatrical treatise is thus rooted in the theory of perspective – and not in the third book on ancient architecture of 1540 dealing with the theatre and the amphitheater.

---

2 The first English translation (Robert Peake, 1611) is based on Coecke's Dutch translation. See Pieter Coecke van Aelst (1606). Here Allardyce Nicoll's modern English translation is used, printed in Hewitt 1958: 24.

3 Cellini (1968 [ca. 1564]: 759) mentions in his contribution to the so-called *Paragone* ('comparison') debates revolving around the priority amongst modes of representation that Serlio planned to publish Leonardo's books on perspective ("Bastiano Serlio, avendo lui volontà di trar fuori questi libri di prospettiva"). Cf. Farago 1992: 26.

4 Serlio's system is also termed *Winkelrahmendekoration*: two horizontal decorated frames are arranged at angles to each other. One frame is positioned parallel to the stage, while the other frame points at an obtuse angle towards an imaginary vanishing point, suggesting spatial depth. In this fashion, the corner of a house is shown; further depiction of staggered corners of buildings creates a perspectivist depiction of a street. This *Winkelrahmendekoration* limits the stage set to its specific genre. It remains unchangeable throughout the performance.

His second book expressly breaks with the rules of the past and hence with the Vitruvian model, portraying a stage "as is the custom in Italy today", that is, "based on perspective" (Serlio 1545: 64). Despite this intermedia approach, he insists on the distinction between panel painting and stage set.

> The general art of perspective we have hitherto considered was concerned with flat planes ('le mura piane') parallel to the front, while this second perspective method is concerned with plastic scenes in relief ('per essere materiale, & di rilievo') (Serlio 1545: 64).[5]

This passage could represent Serlio's contribution to the *paragone* debate. For Leonardo, one of the noblest aspects of painting was *rilievo*, the technique of making an object appear to emerge from the flat surface (Vinci 1882: 394; § 403). The architect Serlio was convinced that the potential for visualization offered by the monumental relief stage with its stable, plastic buildings surpassed the illusionist *rilievo* of painting. In the subsequent period, this distinction between media would be eclipsed: in the semantic evolution that followed Serlio, perspective and scenography became synonymous. Giorgio Vasari's (1511–1574) description of a Roman perspectival stage in his *Life* of Baldassarre Peruzzi (1481–1536) demonstrates this synonymous usage [fig. 3: Perspective set with Roman buildings, mid sixteenth century]:

> But what amazed everyone most was the perspective-view or scenery of a play ('la prospecttiva overo scena d'una comedia'), which was so beautiful that it would be impossible to imagine anything finer, seeing that the variety and beautiful manner of the buildings, the various loggie, the extravagance of the doors and windows, and the other architectural details that were seen in it, were so well conceived and so extraordinary in invention, that one is not able to describe the thousandth part.[6]

Vasari's wording in the second edition of 1568 poses some problems beyond the issue of terminology. He describes a perspectival stage set purportedly created by Peruzzi in 1513 on Rome's Capitol. Today's research claims such a

---

5   This passage is not translated in the first German edition of Serlio's work. See Serlio (1608/09).

6   For the Italian edition and the English translation see Vasari 1976: IV, 320 = Vasari 1996: I, 812.

set never existed at the time in question.⁷ Vasari mentions Serlio as Peruzzi's heir and emulator only in passing: in the second edition of the *Lives*, Serlio's third and fourth book are mentioned, as they are in the first edition of 1550, but he omits the *Libro Secondo*. His familiarity with Serlio's book on perspective is demonstrated elsewhere, in the life of Jacobo Sansovino (1486–1570) of 1568.⁸ Comparison of the two texts reveals that Vasari used Serlio's treatise on the theatre as a template.

Serlio, Libro Secondo (1545: 64ʳ)	Vasari, Vite, BALDASSARRE PERUCCI SANESE (1550/1568: IV, 322-24; 328)
dove si **vede in piccol spacio** fatto dall'arte della Prospettiva, superbi **pallazzi, amplissimi Tempii, diversi casamenti**, & da presso, & di lontano spaciose piazze ornate di varii edificii, dirittissime & lunghe **strade incrociate da altre vie**,archi trionfali,altissime colonne, **piramidi, obelischi**, & mille altre **cose belle,ornate d'infiniti lumi**...Pure quantunque questo modo di Prospettiva, di che io parlerò, sia diuerso dalle regole passate per essere quelle imaginate sopra le mura piane, e questa per essere materiale, o di rilieuo,è ben ragione è tenere altra strada.	[Ed. 1550:] Fece nel tempo di Leone, in Campidoglio di Roma, per recitare una comedia, uno apparato et una prospettiva; nel qual lavoro si mostrò quanto di perfezione e di grazia fosse nell'ingegno di Baldassarre dal cielo infuso: né mai si può pensare di vedere **i palazzi, le case et i tempii** nelle scene moderne **quanto di grandezza mostrasse, nella piccolezza** del sito dall'ingegno di sì gran prospettivo fatto, le stravaganti **bizzarrie di andari in cornici e di vie**, che con case parte vere e finite ingannavano gli occhi di tutti, dimostrandosi esser, **non una piazza dipinta, ma vera**; e quella sì di lumi e di abiti nelle figure de gli istrioni fece propri et al vero simili, che non le favole recitare parevano in comedia, ma una cosa vera e viva, la quale allora intervenisse. [Ed. 1568:] una piazza piena d'archi, colossi, **teatri, obelisci, piramidi, tempii** di diverse maniere [...].

---

7   On the reconstruction of the theatre festival of 1513, cf. Janitschek 1882: 259–70. Contemporary witnesses describe, instead of a perspectival stage, a *scaenae frons*, drawing on the classical Roman theatre. Cf. here Flechsig 1894: 55–56. For all contemporary sources and a commentary, cf.: Cruciani 1969: 80; Lieberman 2005: 149.

8   Vasari 1987: VI, 184 ("simile a quella pianta che Sebastiano Serlio pose nel suo secondo libro di architettura").

The vocabulary and argumentation are largely the same: both texts praise the potential of the perspectival stage to show a large city in a small space. Both texts emphasize the optical persuasion of a spatial depth that is not painted but achieved through plastic design. It is also remarkable that Vasari employs the technical term *bizzaria*, probably first used by Serlio in his third book to describe Egyptian constructions ("bizzarrie Egittie") such as an obelisk that we can perceive in the far distance of his "Tragic Scene" (Serlio 1540: 72; Dethlefs 2018c: 85-86).

In Vasari's narrative, it was Peruzzi who created the new perspectival stage: he "opened the way to those who have since made them in our own day ('apersono la via a coloro che ne hanno poi fatto a' tempi nostri')".[9] Vasari's strategy is not difficult to decode: the highly influential, epoch-making instauration of a type of festival *all'antica* thus coincides with Giuliano and Lorenzo de' Medici's being awarded Roman citizenship in 1513, at the behest of the newly incumbent pope, Leo X, Giovanni de' Medici. Vasari's historical reconstruction is a re-writing of history devised to glorify the Medici. The fact he uses one of Serlio's own texts to diminish the role he played renders it even more remarkable. In his fourth book on the arrangement of columns, which Vasari knew and used (without acknowledgment), Serlio honored his teacher Peruzzi. He briefly discusses the genesis of the perspectival stage, stating that Peruzzi had his predecessors:

> But what should I say on this occasion about the amazing and artificial scenes that were made in Rome by the aforementioned Baldassar? They were all the more laudable because the production costs were lower than the others made before or after.[10]

The Italian historiographer and biographer Paolo Giovio (1483–1552), whose *Vitae virorum illustrium* (around 1527) contains the earliest biography on Leonardo, considers him to have been the inventor of Milan's Court Theatre ("cum elegantiae omnis delitiarumque maxime theatralium mirificus

---

9   Vasari 1967: IV, 323. For the English translation by Gaston De Vere see Vasari 1996: 814. – His attribution is still adhered to by modern theatre historiographers such as Kindermann 1984: I, 161-62; Brauneck 1993: I, 459–60.

10 Serlio 1540 [1537]: 70ʳ: "Ma che dirò io in questa occasione delle stupende e artificiose Scene, fatte in Roma dal detto Baldassar? le quai furono tanto piu degne di lode, quanto fu minore la spesa in farle, delle altre fatte prima di quelle, o dopo ancora". – Cf. Hubertus 1988: 228-29.

inventor ac arbiter esset") (Giovio 2009 [1810]: 20). Whether this meant a perspectival stage in the style of Leonardo's Windsor sketch remains open to conjecture, however. It has been mooted that it was invented by Donato Bramante (1444–1514); an anonymous engraving of a monumental road bears the inscription "Bramanti. Architecti. Opus" [fig. 4: Anon., A street with various buildings, colonnades and an arch. 1475?-1510?] (Flechsig 1894: 92-94).

3. *Wohlstand* and Social Order: Ryff's Rejection of Theatre

Serlio draws on Leonardo's syntagm "in un' solo sguardo" in the extended edition of his *Regole Generali di Architectura*, issued in 1540. Here too, he is interested in the potential of perspective to capture many things at a single glance. In the twelfth chapter of the fourth book, which appeared in German translation by Pieter Coecke van Aelst and Jacob Rechlinger as early as 1542, the decisive passage asserts it is precisely the varied arrangement of groups, figures, foliage etc. that provides a manageable overview without "taxing the eyes"; the observer has to be able to have an overview of "the whole work at a single glance ('mit ayne[m] auge[n]blick das gantz werck'; 'ad vna sola occhiata si comprenda tutta l'opera')."[11]

Serlio's description of enabling the viewer to effortlessly gain an impression of the whole correlates with a key term in his theory of architecture: *commodità* (and the verb and adjective deriving from it, *accommodare, commodo*). The term alludes to one of the main fundamental aesthetic concepts of Vitruvian architecture. For Vitruvius, *commoditas* is part of *ordinatio* in the sense of conveniently proportioned.[12] In Serlio, they gain a new semantic function – utility, comfort, convenience. This is also, indeed especially, related to the modern roofed theatre, which provides comfort insofar as it protects the

---

11   Serlio, Coecke van Aelst [and Rechlinger] 1542a: 69ʳ = Serlio 1540 [1537]: 70ᵛ. – Unlike the faithful, literal German translation, Coecke's French edition – also published in 1542 – deviates from Serlio's original with respect to this important passage. Puttfarken (2000: 258) stated that "*occhiata* does not figure in Italian critism". He overlooked the early Italian uses of the concept in Leonardo and Serlio. See also Puttfarken 1994: 296.
12   On Vitruvius's *commoditas*, cf. Jolles 1906: 10–11; Dethlefs 2011: 102–107; Nagelsmit (2002: 354) is incorrect in his assertion that Serlio's *commodità* had no equivalent in Vitruvius.

audience from inclement weather. In Ryff's German translation of Serlio's second book of 1547, *commoditas* is translated as *Wohlstand*, good order or appearance. The text describes the procedure of dividing a square in such a way that the chessboard-like floor ("pavimento") conveys distance corresponding with the visual pyramid [fig. 5], a technique Serlio employed in his stage sets [fig. 6]. Various figures can be added to this parallelogram "for enjoyment and better appearance ('wolstand')" (Rivius 1547: 14^r [I, part 4]). This corresponds to Serlio's phrasing "accommodare in qualunque quadro che scortia" (Serlio 1545: 29^r). Ryff further uses *Wohlstand* in the ethical sense, as an antonym for "indecency, or impropriety ('unbehörlicheit / oder nit zimung')".[13]

This implicit moral judgement Ryff attaches to the aesthetic concept of *Wohlstand* comes to the fore in his assessment of the theatre: in the German edition of the Second Book, intended to provide "prosperity for utility, and benefit", he omits Serlio's treatise on the theatre. He explains this omission by simply stating that German artisans and architects are not familiar with the theatre and the "spectacle building for various plays" (Rivius 1547: 52^v).[14] They are only found in Italy at the courts of "powerful lords and princes, in great big cities, with lavish great expense, and less utility", serving displays of splendor, "indulgence and delight".[15] He particularly voices disapproval of the use of theatrical machinery to simulate supernatural events:

> Such plays also use various winches and artificial instruments, so that depending on the requirements of the play entire people could be lowered from above, swiftly and without harm, as if the gods were descending from heaven with lightning, thunder and hail, and were whisked back up again in the same fashion [...].[16]

---

13 Rivius 1548: 230^v = Vitruvius VII. v. 6 ("vitium indecentiae"). – Cf. Simon Roth 1571: [51]: „Commoditet, Fůgsamigkait / Fůggschickligkait / Wolstand / komligkeit / dienstwilligkeit."

14 The first German translation of Serlio's treatise on theatre can be found in Ludwig König's 1608/09 Basel Serlio Edition of Books I-V. Cf. Günther 2004: 301-02.

15 Ryff ignores contemporary theatre activities in the German territories and especially in his native town of Strasbourg. See Kindermann 1986: 30-41.

16 Rivius 1547: 52^v: „In solchem schaw spil wurden auch mancherley hebzug und künstliche Instrument gebraucht / damit man zu wegen bringen mocht nach erforderung des spils dz man gantze persone(n) von oben herab lassen mocht / geschwind und on schaden / als ob die Götter von Himel herab stiegen mit Plitz / Donder un(d) Hagel/ und gleicher gestalt widerum verzuckt und ubersich hinauff in die höch gefurt wurden".

The passage paraphrases the section "De' lumi artificiali delle Scene" in the appendix to Serlio's theatre treatise, taken up by Ryff only to voice his disapproval. In this piece, Serlio describes with great enthusiasm innovations in stagecraft such as the ascent and descent of planets, divine figures or the production of thunder and lightning.[17] For Ryff, the possibilities offered by this new stagecraft that played "not only with the saints, but also with Christ's image" were a great evil. Further arguments against the theatre were the cost of construction and upkeep. He condemns the expenses incurred by court theatre lovers in Italy, without naming any names. He was probably referring to the commentary to the first Italian edition of Vitruvius, the *Como Vitruvius* edition of 1521 by the architect and student of Bramante, Cesare Cesariano (1483–1543). The *Como Vitruvius* mentions Duke Ercole I. of Este (1431–1505), who had a theatre built in the courtyard of his palace in Ferrara in 1486, where a Classical comedy was staged – the *Menaechmi* of Plautus (ca. 254–ca.184 B.C.) (Cesariano 1521: 75^r).[18]

A year after berating the theatre, Ryff published his *Vitruvius Teutsch* with commentary (1548). The work demanded he adopt a new stance – at least towards the classical theatre. He does not wish to doubt its exemplary status, interpreting Greek theatre as a school of morals and virtue. While the common people were entertained, this was not "without careful clever teaching on virtue, good morals and punishment of vice".[19] There are many traces of Serlio's theatrical treatise throughout Ryff's commentary. Firstly, this applies to the architectural terminology: Vitruvius uses the term *scaenographia* to denote the reproduction of a façade with optically receding side walls by use of shadow and having all lines correspond to what he described as the center of a circle ("circinique centrum omnium linearum responsus") (Vitruvius I.ii.2) [fig. 7: Ichnographia, orthographia, scaenographia, in: Fra Giovanni Giocondo: Vitruvio, 1511].[20] Ryff, on the other hand, defines *scaenographia* as

---

17 Serlio (1545): 71^V = Hewitt (1958), pp. 35-36: "Thunder, lightning, and thunderbolts will be needed on occasion [...]. Before the thunder has stopped rumbling, the tail of the rocket is discharged, setting fire to the thunderbolt and producing an excellent effect ('mentre si farà lo tuono, nel finir di quello sia scaricata una coda, et nel medesimo tempo dato il fuoco al folgore, & farà buono effetto')."
18 Cf. Torello-Hill 2014: 228–29.
19 Rivius 1548: 166^V ("nit on fursichtige kluge unterrichtung der tugent guter sitten un(d) straffung der laster").
20 Cf. Krause 1985: 50; Tybout 1989: 62-3.

"the display and depiction of the lateral sides in perspectivist fashion" and explicitly interprets Vitruvius' "center of a circle" in the modern sense of a one-point linear perspective. Hence Ryff too uses perspective and scenography as synonyms:

> But there can be no scenography without the perspective of the side walls' recession and tapering, hence such a building is arranged according to the viewpoint [...].[21]

For further explanations, he refers to the "tractetlein der Geometri vnd Perspectiva" in his *Kunstbuch* of 1547, which contains the treatise on the Albertian geometry-based perspective (Rivius 1548: 24^r).

Scaena versatilis and *periactoi* are key terms used by Vitruvius to describe decorative moveable elements on the classical stage. Ryff misunderstands these terms, as demonstrated by his attempt to explain the *periactoi* ("quae loca Graeci *periactus* dicunt ab eo, quod machinae sunt in his locis versatiles trigonos habentes") (Vitruvius V.vi.8).[22] Vitruvius is referring to three-sided upright prisms that are painted or covered with canvas and can be pivoted [fig. 8]. He recommends transforming decorations via the use of *periactoi* when gods appear accompanied by, as he puts it, thunderclaps ("cum tonitribus"). Ryff assumes that the *periactoi* must be the lifting or winding apparatus for vertical stage entries, as described by Serlio.[23] He repeats the disapproval he

---

21 Rivius 1548: 28^V („Aber die Scenographia on die Perspectiva nit beschehen mag/ von der verlierung und abstelung der neben seiten / darumb solcher baw nach den puncten des gesichts gerichtet").
22 Cf. Fiechter 1914: 116–17; Schöne 1933: 17; Little 1936: 407–418; Bieber 1961: 75; Kotte 2013: 193.
23 Rivius 1548: 177^r: "Periactus hat den namen von dem umwenden / dan(n) an solchem ort waren Hebzeug so man Machinas nennet / dardurch [...] mit solchem zug mocht man auch die Götter ab unnd auff lassen". – This misunderstanding can also be found in Antonio da Sangallo the Younger, who also links the problem of periaktoi to the appearance of gods: "Triangulare machina, quale si gira secondo li efetti della comedia, per che in ogni facia a varij efetti, cioè in una l'aparatione Dei". Sangallo's autograph note is printed in Milanesi's edition of Vasari's *Lives* (1906: V, 519). The same holds for the translation of Vitruvius produced by Fabio Calvo ca. 1513 under the supervision of Raphael (in: Calvo 1975 [ca. 1513]: 218): periaktoi are "machine sostengono trigoni versatile", each having three decorations ("ornamenti") that change with the story ("quando se haveva a mutar fibula"). Here too, a change of scene is required when Jupiter enters with his thunderclap. Calvo and Raphael are uncertain regarding the positioning of the periaktoi, which are to stand "near" the aula regia (the central

Perspectival Stage and German Reception of *Second Book of Architecture* (1545)   57

voiced in his Serlio translation: thunder should be avoided, since it is evocative of "dark Judas masses ('finster Judas Metten')" (Rivius 1548: 177 ʳ). Presumably Ryff had never seen a transformative stage: his image of the classical theatre stage is informed by Serlio's modern idea of a demarcated, predetermined, unchanging space rooted in the central perspective, the audience having a fixed location and an unchanging view.

Serlio's third book contains the outline of what Ryff would present as the Colosseum in Rome [fig 9: Rivius: Vitruvius Teutsch, 1548. Fig. 10: Serlio, Il terzo libro, 1540].[24] The reason why Ryff – unlike Jean Martin († 1553) in his French Vitruvius translation of 1547 – omits Serlio's three suggestive stage sets is easy to explain.[25] The comedic stage set shows front right the house of *Rufia*, the bawd of a municipal brothel, which is difficult to reconcile with Ryff's theory of the classical theatre as a school of virtue [fig. 11: Serlio, setting for comedy, Secondo libro 1545] (Krautheimer 1988: 337).

He provides detailed comment on the seating plan in the classical theatre, particularly with respect to the seats of honor for Augustus ("des Keyers Augusti") and the senators in the orchestra's half-circle (Rivius 1548: 177 ʳ). Remarkably, Ryff compares them to the choir stalls of Christian churches. He claims the practice was to

> put in such places chairs and ornamental seats that were taken away again after such plays were over, although over time they were allocated here permanently, as is the custom in today's churches, where the choir stalls are built permanently, and everyone has his own set place according to his status [...].[26]

---

palace gate) and the hospitalia (the entrances to the guests' quarters on the left and right) ("apresso a questi spazii siano facti").

24   Together with Philandrier's *Les annotations sur le De Architectura de Vitruve* (Rome 1544), Rivius's Latin Vitruvius edition printed in Strasbourg (1543: 96, 99, 100) is one of the earliest examples in which Serlio's illustrations are used. Cf. Serlio 1537: 6ʳ. Cf. Röttinger 1914: 18.

25   Klein / Zerner (1964: 53, n.14) incorrectly state that Ryff used Serlio's stage sets in his *Vitruvius Teutsch*.

26   Rivius 1548: 174ᵛ: „und pflag man Sessel und zierliche sitz an solche ort zu stellen / die man nach vollendung solcher spil widerum hinweg nam / wie wol mit der zeit auch die selbigen zu ewiger werung hernach auch hieher geordnet wurden / wie dann noch diser zeit in unsern Kirchen der brauch / da man die stül im Chor ewig bleibend bawet /unnd nach ordnung der dignitet ein yeder sein steten platz hat".

Perhaps this passage contains vestiges of the combination of theatrical performance and Christian service in Cesariano ("como faceno li solemni e Divini officii, con soni e cantici affigurati"), also found in Leonardo's MS B [fig. 12: Leonardo da Vinci, "teatro da predicare", ca. 1487-89, Paris] (Cesariano 1521: 75ʳ).[27] It also features in Cesariano's graphic reconstruction of a classical theatre building, which is reminiscent of a Christian baptistery [fig. 13: Cesare Cesariano, Monopteral temple from *Como Vitruvius* 1521].

4. *Thematismos/Statio* – The Site of the Roman Theatre, its Political and Symbolic Function

The topographical connection between the theatre building and the temple is a characteristic of many Roman theatres [fig. 14: The Theatre of Pompeius with temple of Venus Victrix, Rome, according to the third century C.E. Severan marble plan] (Brauneck 1993: I, p. 213; Kolb 2010: 132). According to Vitruvius, the construction of public and cult buildings strictly observes décor "cum auctoritate et ratione decoris" – "with proper *wolstand*", in Ryff's translation.[28] Vitruvius uses a threefold definition of *decor(um)* according to the criteria of *thematismos*, *consuetudo* and *natura*. The first of these terms demands closer attention: Greek *tò théma* means that which has been set, established, or imposed, a law, a statute, usage, the latter also in the sense of having something at one's disposal (Passow 1847: 1135). *Thematismos* is a grammatical or rhetorical term denoting a wide range of phenomena related to art, especially in the field of music [29] – it was rarely used in Antiquity.[30] Vitruvius clearly intended

---

27 Leonardo shows the fusion of theatre and church: a rectangular building divided into three knaves with an apse on both sides, enclosed by a semi-circular theatre with tiered seating and a pulpit in the middle. To the left of the sketch, Leonardo writes: "teatro da predicare" ('theatre for prayer'), in: Vinci 1883: II, 52ʳ. Cf. Marotti 1974: 20, 108.

28 See Rivius 1548: 230ᵛ und „Den Hochgelehrten Fürsichtigen Erbarn vnd Weisen Herren / Bürgermeistern" [unpag. dedication] = Vitruvius VII. v. 4.

29 For *thematismos* as a term belonging to medieval Byzantine music theory see Wellesz 1961: 296; Amargianakis 1977: 75.

30 In Quintilian's *Institutio oratoria* (4. 2. 28) published around year 95 A.D. *themata* is used in the sense of tasks given to pupils in school. There is clearly another classical use of *thematismos*, in the first book of *Adversus Mathematicos* by Sextus Empiricus from the second century A.D. – David L. Blank's Sextus commentary in his text edition of *Sextus Empiricus, Against Grammarians* (1998: 149) is pioneering; to my knowledge, Blank provides the first historical-critical explanation of the term. The sections in which Blank

to establish a formal system of classification serving a hard and fast rule regarding formations consisting of words, sounds or images, in contrast to natural formations. The fact that Vitruvius introduces *thematismos* in connection with the three types of temples suggests he was advancing genre theory: in Book I.2 he uses the term to denote the three *genera* of temples and expressly writes of a "corinthio genere" (Vitruvius I. ii. 5; V. iv. 3; V. vi. 9). This genre triad also features twice in the fifth book: first in the chapter on theory of music with respect to the three *genera* of modulation, Harmonia, Chroma and Diatonon ("Genera vero sunt modulationum tria"), and then when he introduces the three dramatic genres, tragedy, comedy, and the satyr play ("Genera autem sunt scaenarum tria: unum quod dicitur tragicum, alterum comicum, tertium satyricum") (Vitruvius V. iv. 3; V. vi. 9). Vitruvius's Latin translation of *thematismos* is *statio*. Ryff correctly translates *statio* as *Stellung*, "position" or "standing", thus including the figurative meaning of dignity and rank.[31] In contrast to *thematismos*, which denotes having the quality of an artefact, *statio* is a topographical term. It describes places, especially social spaces with specific forms of encounter, experience and acting. As we know from the groundbreaking study by Koestermann (1932: 358–368; 430-444), as *statio principis* it represents a constitutional concept describing the purportedly sacred hegemonic practices of the Augustan Principate.[32] The expression is of military derivation, initially referring to army formation and encampment, and was also used more generally to denote a sentry, i.e., someone who keeps his position. *Statio principis* is the place whence a prince keeps watch over the prosperity with which he has been entrusted by his fellow citizens and creates confidence in the stability of the state and trust in its leader. A spatial position, then, is used to refer to conditions of observation implying courses of action and assignments. This space is public; it is a place of assembly distinct from the private *domus*. The diverse *stations* listed by Vitruvius and his contemporaries constitute a topography of sociocultural encounters that primarily refer to buildings and sites of public representation. The connection to the theatre is unequivocally expressed in Juneval's (late 1st – early 2nd century A.D.) eleventh satire

---

elaborates on Vitruvius's wording are less persuasive, not least because he omits *statio*. Cf. also Wehnert 1966: XIII, 282.

31   Vitruvius I. ii.5 = Rivius 1548: 25^r; 31^r.

32   Koestermann's work has influenced many historical studies. Cf. Béranger 1953: 184–86; Bruun 1989: 127–147; Nelis-Clément 2006: 271; France / Nelis-Clément 2014; Benoist 2007: 266; for Gros (2001: 108) *stationes* are administrative seats (*atrium, tabularium, praefectura*).

("thermae, stationes, omne theatrum"). The theatre is the place of encounter between the *princeps* and the people, where universal consensus is expressed in the form of acclamation (Bollinger 1969; Zanker 2003: 151–52; Gros 1987: 319–46). In his elegies, Ovid (43 B.C. – 17 A.D.) describes the *statio* of the *princeps* as the place of the highest power, namely Jupiter's throne, whence he casts his worried eye over the world.[33] Under Augustus, whom Ovid addresses as Jupiter, the theatre advances to the privileged site where political opinion is made and expressed, as established in the third *Tristia*: "The stage is full of life, and partisanship ablaze with warring passions, and three theatres roar in the place of three forums."[34] Horace (65 – 8 B.C.) strongly disapproves of this development in his Epistle to Augustus; he registers tumult among the audience and asks: "For what voices have ever prevailed to drown the din with which our theatres resound?"[35] Horace's recommendation to the audience is that they should first learn to listen.

Vitruvius's lexical correlation *thematismos/statio* merges formal and topographical aspects. *Statio* is primarily used with reference to public buildings constructed "in the open air without a roof" to render visible the appearance and workings of the gods "in open and light-filled space ('horum enim deorum et species et effectus in aperto mundo atque lucenti praesentes vidimus')" (Vitruvius I.ii.5). He is referring here to temples, but the passage also provides an explanation for the openness of the classical theatre. In the theory of decorum, the function of *statio* is to reinforce, through the nature of the place, the authority and dignity ("ex natura loci maiores auctasque cum dignitate divinitas excipiat opiniones") of which the gods are deserving (Vitruvius I.ii.7). Further, the topographical *statio* appears as a "guardhouse" in Book 2.8 and as an "anchoring ground" in Book 5.12. In Book 5.11, Ryff uses the Latin term *stationes*. Here it refers to the seats and resting places along a sycamore-lined avenue leading to a gymnasium. Drawing on Plinius, Ryff interprets these sites as places of conversation, meditation or devotion modelled on the sycamore avenues of the Philosophical Academy in Athens ("walkways of the Philosophical

---

33   Ovid, Trist. II. 217–19 ("Ioui, de te pendentem sic dum circumspicis orbem, effugiunt curas inferiora tuas. Scilicet inperii princeps statione relicta [...].") = Ovid 1953: 71 ("Shouldst thou, forsooth, the prince of the world, abandon thy post [...]?").
34   Ovid: Trist. III. xii. 23-24 ("Scaena uiget studiisque fauor distantibus ardet, / proque tribus resonant terna theatra foris") = Ovid 1953: 149.
35   Horace, Epist. II. i. 200–201 ("Nam quae pervincere voces evaluere sonum, referunt quem nostra theatre") = Horace 1978: 413.

Academy").³⁶ Of particular significance are the several instances of *stationes* in Book 9.1 – with reference to the topography of the heavens. Here he writes of how the planets appear to stand still.

> But Mercury and Venus, their paths wreathing around the sun's rays as their centre, retrograde and delay their movements, and so, from the nature of that circuit wait at stopping-places ('stationibus') within the spaces of the signs.³⁷

The *statio planetae*, i.e., the apparent slower and quicker periodical forward, backward and arrested motion of the planets, is based on ancient observations, according to which a planet appears to remain at a point of the zodiac for some days when viewed from the Earth, which Ptolemy (ca. 100-ca. 180 AD) was first to represent geometrically (Zedler 1744: XL, 106-107, Hepperger 1921: 217; Balss 1949: 151, 272). This idea of temporary planetary arrest becomes the principal meaning of *statio* in Cesariano's Vitruvius commentary: he interprets all of its uses as brief stations: "Statione si e loco unde si li sta per qualche tempo ma non al continuo" (Cesariano 1521: 17ᵛ).³⁸ This represents something

---

36 Rivius 1548: 189ʳ; *Plinius, Nat.hist.* 12.2–5. – Tertullian (ca. 155–230 A.D.), who vehemently condemned the theatre for endangering good morals and its proximity to heathen god cults in *De Spectaculis*, written in Carthage around 200, uses *statio* in many positive variants: for military sentries, places of assembly, offices, and the powers of the gods (*Apolog. II.6; III.6; XI.4*). In *De Ieiunio* (X.1), he breaks with the semantic tradition and uses the term in the sense of Lent to begin the history of Roman stational liturgy, which would soon be followed by many urban architectural measures. On the semantics of *statio* in Christian liturgy, cf. Teeuwen 1926: 112–20; Mohrmann 1953: 221–245; Baldovin 1987: 143–45; Blaaw 1993: 77–86. On *sacre rappresentazioni*, "tableaux vivants", and the Stations of the Cross as prototypes of the early modern theatre, cf. Pochat 1990: 150–54.
37 Vitruvius IX.i.6 ("Mercuri autem et Veneris stellae circa solis radios uti per centrum eum itineribus coronantes regressus retrorsus et retardatione faciunt, etiam stationibus propter eam circinationem morantur in spatiis signorum") = Vitruvius 1960 [1918]: 259.
38 Modern literature on Vitruvius tends to omit the topographical element that was still evident in Vitruvius commentaries of the sixteenth century: in the German-speaking world, *statio* is usually translated as "Satzung" (statute): Jolles 1906: 34; Schlikker 1940: 96; Fensterbusch 1976: 39. Horn-Oncken (1967: 30) uses "Festsetzung" in the sense of "following the habitual, adaptation to nature". Here, *statio, consuetudo, natura* are all interpreted in a similar sense of strict adherence to rules. The French translations are similar here: Fleury, in his translation of the first book (Paris 2003), uses "règle" as in Fleury / Callebat 1995: 63: "règle, principe". A semantic overlap can be found between *statio* and *consuetudo* in the Anglo-Saxon literature: Granger (1931: I, 29) uses "conven-

of a shift in the semantic perspective. Vitruvius opens all ten books of the work with eulogies to Augustus, suggesting he interprets the topographical *statio* against the background of the constitutional *statio principis*. Such an interpretation would have consequences: it is not just the nature of the place that defines the decorum; rather it is the *princeps* who makes demands and by virtue of his position watches over decorum, order, and compliance with rules. This possible interpretation is supported by the fact that the predicate *auctoritas* Augustus claims for himself in his account of his deeds *Res gestae* ("mea auctoritate deductas") is also the predicate of Vitruvius's *statio*.[39] Cesariano, on the other hand, ignores the function of politico-cultural depictions of hegemony in favour of a cosmological meaning. His interpretation was not without its impact: he was echoed by later Italian Vitruvius commentators of the early Cinquecento as well as by the German commentator Ryff.[40]

Cesariano illustrates these cosmological references in his drawing of the Vitruvian theatre's floor plan: the circular plan is inscribed with four equilateral triangles, the points of which meet the circular line in twelve equal intervals. In a paragraph modern Vitruvius scholars consider to be later textual interpolation,[41] the twelve equal sections of the circle are said to symbolise the twelve signs of the zodiac ("von den Astrologis in der bezeichnung

---

tion" for *statio*. This interpretation is also adopted by Payne 1999: 37–38. Watzinger (1909: 216), who understands *statio* as a concept in its own right, connected to "certain immutable demands" made by the inhabitant of a building and corresponding to his ethical profile, anticipates Koestermann's findings.

39   Augustus, *Res Gestae* 28. – A further argument is that *thematismos* and *statio* can only be equivalent if we have *princeps*. Again, we must draw on Blank's commentary on *thematismos* in Sextus. Blank (1998: 182) identifies two uses of the conjugation *thematizō* – in Sextus and in the epicurean philosopher Philodemos (110–ca.40–35 B.C.). Both use it in the sense of to "set up in a primary position". Dictionaries define *princeps* as "One who, or that which, is first, foremost". Derivations include prince, principal, and principle. Hence once might speak of a hidden equivalence of *thematismos* and *statio (principis)* in Vitruvius.

40   Calvo (1975 [ca. 1513]: 10ʳ) uses *statio* in connection with the topography of the heavens: "se fa con stazione e firmamento, lo quale in greco se dice *thematismos*". Caporali (1536: 21ʳ) relies heavily on Cesariano: "Statione, è luocho dove per qualque tempo altri dimora, ma non per lo contineuo come sono anchora le navi in alchun porto: ponsi anchora questo nome STATIO per lo constituito ordine de li di, & anchora per molte altre significationi, come per quei luochi dove le guardie de la notte si pongono".

41   Fensterbusch 1964: 551 (n. 278). See also Saliou's commentary (Vitruve 2009: 223-26).

der zwelff Hymlischen zeichen auß der vergleichung des gestirns mit der Musica").[42] Ryff adopted Cesariano's focus on a cosmological organising principle [fig. 15: Ryff: Vitruvius Teutsch, Cesariano Vitruvius-Como: design scheme of a theater ground plan]. He writes of the distribution that stems "from the astrologers' denoting the twelve celestial signs by comparing the constellation to music". Music functions as a copula uniting the topography of the theatre with the topography of the heavens. Numerical architectural proportions are like musical intervals corresponding to a harmonic cosmic law. What, Ryff asks in his commentary, is musical harmony other than "an earthly-heavenly spirit ('ein Elementischer hymlischer Geyst') that moves harmoniously in the same order and proportion heaven, earth and all creatures?"[43] This passage echoes the *Como Vitruvius*. Cesariano calls this correspondence *concinnità* ("con la concinitare & per interualli") – an expression one will not find in Vitruvius's vocabulary (Cesariano 1521: 76ʳ). The term denotes the accord between the upper and lower world ("spirito elementale & celeste") (Cesariano 1521: 76ʳ). Cesariano may have borrowed the expression from Marsilio Ficino's commentary on the Platonic *Convivium*: here *concinnitas* and *inconcinnitas* denote a hidden natural harmony or disharmony: when the shape of an object agrees with its representation in the mind, attraction, or fondness results. The *concinnitas* produces in the lines and colours of the physical world, in education and behaviour, a certain splendour and sparkle (*splendor, fulgor*) which for Ficino are only perceptible to the eye.[44]

Ryff was familiar with the term *concinnitas* from translating Alberti's *De pictura*. With respect to the new perspectives in history painting, Ryff translates *concinnitas* as *Wohlstand*.[45] Ryff's translation, informed by connotations

---

42   Rivius 1548: 174ʳ = Vitruvius V.vii.6 ("quibus etiam in duodecim signorum caelestium astrologia ex musica convenientia astrorum ratiocinantur").
43   Rivius 1548: 169ʳ ("dann was mag das lieblich gethȇn und sȗß zusamen stymmung oder Concent Musicalischer Harmoni anders geschetzt werden / dann ein Elementischer hymlischer Geyst / so in gleicher ordnung und proportion / wie Hymel / Erden / und alle Geschöpff mit maß und zal in gebürlicher mensur getriben und bewegt / solchen lieblichen Concent die wunderwerck Gottes anzeigen").
44   Ficino, *De amore*, 5. 5; 2. 9 ("Nempe corporis pulchritudo nihil aliud est quam splendor ipse in colorum linearumque decore. Animi quoque pulchritudo, fulgor in doctrine et morum concinnitate").
45   Rivius 1547: 24ᵛ ("Accord of mood and pleasantness [...] in equal harmony" ("enharmonicum concentum in musicis instrumentis"). – Dethlefs 2007: 143–155; Dethlefs, 2011: 130-35; Dethlefs 2018a: 131-37; Dethlefs 2018b: 240-45.

from Vitruvius, Alberti and Serlio, implies a comprehensive system of order and salvation. He holds that this system is perceptible to the naked eye via the new perspective. He compares the central perspective's perceptual process with Jupiter's thunderbolt, which suddenly bursts from the clouds "as if golden rain were scattering golden hail drops all around ('als ob der Guldin rege[n] mit guldenen hagel tröpfflin die gantze gegnet vberspreite')" (Rivius 1547: 37^r).

5. Audience Behavior: The Theatre's Role in Forging Identity and Community

The seventh chapter of Alberti's eighth book on architecture, first printed in 1485, is entitled "On the furnishings of play and theatres houses, and their utility". For Alberti, their utility, indeed their indispensability lies in their ability to forge a harmonious, supportive community among the residents of a city. He thereby foregrounds their socio-political function: the community should assemble on feasts with the aim to calm "the tempers via these meetings and communal meals" and promote friendship between fellow citizens ("ad amicitiae fructum paratiores redder") (Alberti 1966 [1485]: 724).

While Ryff sees no social benefit in contemporary theatre, he recognises that civil society encounters serve to forge identity and community, helping members of related professions share their views: musicians, doctors and astrologists enjoy "communion" with one another; the "liberal arts" come into contact with "geometry", geometry with *perspektiva*, "which Vitruvius called optice ('die Geometri mit der Perspectiva / welche von Vitruvio Optice genant wirt')" (Rivius 1548: 24^r).[46] Debate within these communities is held in relation to one's profession, with a cosmological orientation, an "astronomical comparison of viewpoints ('Astronomische vergleichung der Aspect')" (Rivius 1548: 23^r). Ryff makes these remarks in his commentary on Vitruvius' catalogue of disciplines of architectural training. Here he develops an idea that could have been productive, namely freeing *comparison, vergleichung* or *paragone* from the context of competition and rivalry that dominated the Italian debate in favor

---

46   Vitruvius does not equate perspective (or *scaenographia*) and optics. As an early example of expressions such as "Optica sive Perspectiva" in medieval optics, Ineinchen (1985: 21) cites the late 12th-century translation of the Ptolemaic optics from Arabic into Latin.

of a collegial pooling of knowledge and knowledge networking.[47] Ryff misses the opportunity to advance this argument, since he cannot offer a place of assembly and encounter for interdisciplinary dialogues. With respect to the perception of professional groups in the public sphere, he overlooks an interesting transitional phenomenon in the history of the theatre, to which I would like to draw further attention in my closing remarks.

In 1543, Andreas Vesalius's ground-breaking anatomical work *De humani corporis fabrica* appeared. Ryff made extensive use of this work in his medical writings.[48] The book's frontispiece shows an anatomical theatre designed by Jan Stephan van Calcar (1499–1546), a pupil of Titian.[49] This is a rare early modern illustration of a theatre in which the audience's behavior is fixed. Here, anatomical necropsy is a social event and stimulus for debate among the assembled spectators [fig. 16: Andreas Vesalius: De humani corporis fabrica (frontispice). 1543]. Calcar's template derives from an early edition of the comedies of the Roman playwright Terence (ca. 195/185– ca. 159 B.C.) which Soardi printed in Venice in 1497 and re-used in an edition of Plautus in 1511 [fig. 17: Plautus, Comedies, 1511]. From the unusual perspective of an actor on the stage of a theatre based on the Roman Colosseum, we see spectators in lively discussion. These early modern spectators are not entertained or passive recipients. They are alert, focused participants involved in passionate exchange – they are, then, *in statione*, in *position* or taking a *stance*. This stance is stronger than modern 'engagement' since it is oriented around duties and professional actions.

---

47 Community building depends on a professional elite for Ryff. On participation in public life see Schalk 1955: 23; Martines 1963: 39-50.
48 On this point see my forthcoming paper on Ryff's Pliny commentary (Dethlefs, forthcoming).
49 In his writings on anatomy, Ryff had already borrowed illustrations from Andreas Vesalius's *Tabulae Sex* (1538); cf. Rivius 1541: 104^v. – In 1551, a Nuremberg surgeon translated Vesal's work under the title *Anatomia zu deudsch – ein kurtzer Aufzug der beschreibung aller glider menschlichs Leybs*. The first anatomical theatres were built in Basel in 1588, Padua in 1594 and Leiden in 1597.

Appendix

	Uses of *statio* in Vitruvius, Ovid and other Latin authors	
Ruler's residence, ruler's position, hegemonic practice	Vitr. I.2: **Statione, cum Iovi Fulguri ... aedificia ... constituentur** ----- Ovid, *Tristia*: **Inperii princeps statione relicta**	Augustus, Epist. ad Gaium, *id salvis nobis traducere liceat in statu reipublicae felicissimo ... stationem meam.* Tacitus, Dial. 17, *adice ... sextam iam felicis huius principatus stationem, qua Vespasianus rem publicam fovet:* Plinius Sec., Panegyricus VII, **Assumptus es in laborum curarumque consortium, nec te laeta et prospera stationis istius, sed aspera et dura ad capessendam eam compulerunt.** Velleius, Hist. Rom. II.124: **pugnantis cum Caesare senatus populique Romani, ut stationi paternae succederet;** II.131: **hunc principem, eique functo longissima statione mortali destinate successores quam serissimos,** Helius I.1: **Diocletiane Auguste, tot principum maxime, non solum eos, qui principum locum in hac statione, quam temperas,** Lampr. Comm. 1.8: **iam in his artifex (sc. Commodus) quae stationis imperatoriae non erant, ut calices fingeret, saltaret, cantaret** [...]. Sueton, Claudius 38.3: **ad susceptam stationem non fuerit**

	Uses of *statio* in Vitruvius, Ovid and other Latin authors		
Guardhouse, sentry, "lifetime post" Office	*Vitr. II.8:* **circa eum locum aedificium struxerunt et id erecta Graia statione texerunt**		*Seneca, Ep. CXX 18,* **Magnus animus dat operam, ut in hac statione, qua positus est, honeste se atque industrie great,**
	Ovid, Fasti V: **Martis opus iuvenes animosaque bella gerebant, et pro dis aderant in statione suis;** *Fasti II:* **qua positus fueris in statione, mane**		*Livius, Urb. Cond. VIII.8:* **praeterquam quod custodiae vigiliaeque et ordo stationum intentioris ubique curae errant** *Sueton, Aug.:* **Centuriones statione deserta,** *Tacitus, Hist. I:* **Stationem in castris agebat [...] quae in Palatio stationem agebat,**
Seat, place of public assembly for conversation, observation, reading, consultation etc.	*Vitr. V.11:* **in his perficiantur inter arbores ambulationes ibique ex opere signino stationes**		*Plin., Hist. Nat. 16:* **stationes municipiorum** *Plin. Sec., Epist. I.13:* **Plerique in stationibus sedent tempusque audiendi fabulis conterunt.**
	Ovid, Trist. III.1: **Caesar, ades voto, maxime diue, meo. Interea, quoniam statio mihi publica clausa est, privato liceat delituisse loco.**		*Plin. Sec., Epist. II:* **prenso amicos, supplico, ambio, domos stationesque** *Juvenal, Satirae XI:* **omnis convictus, thermae, stationes, omne theatrum.** *Tertullian, Apol.III.6:* **Etiam a locis conventiculorum et stationum suarum Stoici, Academici?**
Anchor ground, mooring, harbour; refuge	*Vitr. V.12:* **si nullum flumen in his locis inpedierit sed erit ex una parte statio** *Ovid, Met. VII:* **fluctibus eiectum tuta statione recepi**		*Virgil, Aenaeid II.23:* **Nunc tantum sinus et statio male fida carinis; Huc se provecti deserto in litore condunt.** *Sueton, Tiberius:* **statione per ripas Tiberis** *Velleius, Hist. Rom. II.72:* **tempestatem fugientibus statio pro portu foret.**

Planetary standstill	Vitr. IX.6: **stationibus propter eam circinationem morantur in spatiis signorum.** ---------- Ovid, Fasti V.720: **alterna fratrem statione redemit:** utile sollicitae sidus utrumque rati Ovid, Met. II: **diffugiunt stellae, quarum agmina cogit Lucifer et caeli statione novissimus exit.**	Plinius, Hist. Nat. II.15: **Veneris stella et stationes duas, matutinam verspertinamque, ab utroque exortu facit a longissimis distantiae suae finibus, Mercurii stationum breviore momento quam ut deprehendi possint.** Lukrez, De rerum nat. IV: **solque pari ratione manere et luna videtur in statione,** Manilius, Astronomicon III, 76: **in æterna coeli statione manerent**

References

Alberti, Leon Battista (1966): De re aedificatoria, Orlandi, Giovanni/Portoghesi, Paolo (eds.). Milano: Il Polifilo.

Amargianakis George (1977): An analysis of stichera in the Deuteros modes: the stichera idiomela for the month of September in the modes Deuteros, Plagal Deuteros, and Nenano; transcribed from the Manuscript Sinai 1230, A.D. 1365, Copenhagen: University of Copenhagen.

Augustus (1975): Res Gestae /Tatenbericht, Monumentum Ancyranum, Stuttgart: Reclam.

Baldovin, Francis (1987): The Urban Character of Christian Worship: The Origins, Development, and Meaning of Stational Liturgy, Rome: Pontifical Oriental Institute Press.

Balss, Heinrich (1949): Antike Astronomie. Munich: Heimeran.

Benoist, Stéphane (2007): L'identité du prince face à la crise: construction d'un discours et usage de la memoria", in: Olivier Hekster et al. (eds.), Crises and the Roman Empire: Proceedings of the Seventh Workshop [...], Leiden/Boston: Brill, pp. 261–74.

Béranger, Jean (1953): Recherches sur l'aspect idéologique du principat. Basel: Impr. Reinhardt.

Bieber, Margarete (1961), History of the Greek and Roman Theater, Princeton: Princeton Univ. Press.

Blaaw, Sible de (1993): Het ideaal van de stad als kerk. Verwal en herleving van de Romeinse statieliturgie, in: Bouwkunst. Studies voor Kees Peeters, Amsterdam: Architectura & Natura Pers. pp. 77–86.

Blank, David L. (1998): Sextus Empiricus: Against the Grammarians (Adversus Mathematicos I), Oxford: Clarendon Press.

Bollinger, Traugott (1969): Theatralis Licentia. Die Publikumsdemonstrationen an den öffentlichen Spielen im Rom der früheren Kaiserzeit und ihre Bedeutung im politischen Leben, Winterthur: Hans Schellenberg.

Brauneck, Manfred (1993): Die Welt als Bühne. Geschichte des europäischen Theaters, Stuttgart/Weimar: Metzler.

Bruun, Christer (1989): Statio aquarum, in: Lacus Iuturnae I (Lavori e studi di archeologia 12), pp. 127–147.

Calvo, Fabio (1975 [ca. 1513]): Vincenzo Fontana et.al. (eds.), Vitruvio e Raffaello. Il De architettura di Vitruvio nella traduzione inedita di Fabio Calvo ravennate, Rome: Officina ed.

Caporali, Giovanni Battista (1536): Architettvra: con il svo cōmento et figvre Vetrvvio in volgar lingva raportato per M. Gianbatista Caporali de Pervgia, Perugia: Bigazzini.

Cellini, Benedetto (1968 [ca. 1564]): Sopra la differenza nata tra gli scultori e pittori circa il luogo destro dato alla Pittura nelle esequie del gran Michelangiolo Buonarroti, in Opere, ed. Bruno Maier, Milano: Rizzoli.

Cesariano Cesare (1969 [1521]): De architectura libri dece: traducti de latino in vulgare, affigurati, cōmentati, & con mirando ordine insigniti: per il quale facilmente potrai trouare la multitudine de li abstrusi & reconditi vocabuli a li soi loci & in epsa tabula con summo studio expositi & enucleati ad immensa utilitate de ciascuno studioso & beniuolo di epsa opera, Repr. of the Como-edition of 1521 with an introd. and index by Carol Herselle Krinsky, Munich: Fink.

Cruciani, Fabrizio (1969): II Teatro del Campidoglio e le Feste Romane del 1513, Milan: Il Polifilo.

Dethlefs, Hans Joachim (2007): Wohlstand and Decorum in the German 16th-Century Art Theory. in: Journal of the Warburg and Courtauld Institutes 70, pp. 143–155.

Dethlefs, Hans Joachim (2011): Der Wohlstand der Kunst, Tokyo: Chuo University Press.

Dethlefs, Hans Joachim (2018a): Convenience/Decorum, in: Michèle-Caroline Heck (ed.), LexArt. Words for Painting (France, Germany, England,

The Netherlands, 1600-1750), Montpellier: Presses universitaires de la Méditerranée, pp.131-37.

Dethlefs, Hans Joachim (2018b): Harmony, in: Michèle-Caroline Heck (ed.), LexArt. Words for Painting (France, Germany, England, The Netherlands, 1600-1750), Montpellier: Presses universitaires de la Méditerranée, pp. 240-45.

Dethlefs, Hans Joachim (2018c): Caprice / Bizarreness, in: Michèle-Caroline Heck (ed.), LexArt. Words of Painting (France, Germany, England, The Netherlands, 1600-1750), Montpellier: Presses universitaires de la Méditerranée, pp. 85-91.

Dethlefs, Hans Joachim (forthcoming): Sur l'imagination et la fascination dans un commentaire allemand de Pliny du XVIe siècle, In Elizabeth Claire, Béatrice Delaurenti, Roberto Poma, Koen Vermeir (eds), Le corps et les pouvoirs de l'imagination, Paris: EHESS.

Farago, Claire J. (1992): Leonardo da Vinci's Paragone. A critical interpretation with a new edition of the text in the Codex Urbinas, Leiden: Brill.

Fiechter, Ernst Robert (1914): Die baugeschichtliche Entwicklung des antiken Theaters, Munich: Beck.

Flechsig, Eduard (1894): Die Dekoration der modernen Bühne in Italien. Von den Anfängen bis zum Schluß des 16. Jahrhunderts, Dresden: Schulze.

Fleury, Philippe, Callebat, Louis (1995): Dictionnaire des termes techniques du De architectura de Vitruve, Hildesheim: Olms.

Frey, Dagobert (1946): Kunstwissenschaftliche Grundfragen, München: Rohrer-Verl.

Giovio, Paolo (2009): Leonardi Vincii Vita, in: Giuseppe Bossi: Del Cenacolo di Leonardo da Vinci (1810), Milan: Skira 2009.

Gros, Pierre (1987): La fonction symbolique des édifices théâtraux dans le paysage de la Rome augustéene", in: L'urbs; espace urbain et histoire. Collection de l'école française de Rome, Paris: Boccard, pp. 319–46.

Gros, Pierre (2001): Les édifices de la bureaucratie impériale: administration, archives et services publics dans le centre monumental de Rome, Pallas 55, pp. 107–26.

Günther, Hubertus (1988): Das geistige Erbe Peruzzis im vierten und dritten Buch des Sebastiano Serlio, in: Jean Guillaume (ed.), Les traités d architecture de la Renaissance, Paris: Picard, pp. 227-245.

Günther, Hubertus (2004): „L'édition en allemande des livres I à V chez Ludwig König à Bale en 1608 et 1609, in: Sylvie Deswarte-Rosa (ed.), Sebastiano Serlio a Lyon. Architecture & Imprimerie, Roanne: SRI Édition, pp. 301-02.

Hewitt, Barnard (1958): The Renaissance stage. Documents of Serlio, Sabbattini and Furttenbach, Miami: Univ. of Miami Press.

Horn-Oncken, Alste (1967): Über das Schickliche. Studien zur Geschichte der Architekturtheorie. Göttingen: Vandenhoeck & Ruprecht.

Horace (1978): Satires, Epistles and Ars Poetica, H. Rushton Fairclough (ed., trans.) London/ Cambridge MA: Harvard Univ. Press.

Ineinchen, Gustav (1985): La prospettiva: identificazione di un termine, in: Clemens Krause (ed.), La prospettiva pittorica: un convegno, Roma: Istituto Svizzero, pp. 19-23.

Jacquot, Jean (1964): Les types de lieu théâtral et leurs transformations de la fin du Moyen Age au milieu du XVIIe siècle", in: Jean Jacquot (ed.): Le lieu théâtral a la Renaissance, Paris: Editions du Centre National de la Recherche Scientifique, pp. 474–83.

Janitschek, Hubert (1882): Das kapitolinische Theater im Jahre 1513, in: Repert. für Kunstwissenschaft 5, pp. 259–70.

Johnson, Eugene J. (2018): Inventing the Opera House: Theater Architecture in Renaissance and Baroque Italy, Cambridge: Cambridge University Press.

Jolles, André (1906): Vitruvs Ästhetik, Diss. Freiburg 1906.

Kindermann, Heinz (1959): Theatergeschichte Europas, Salzburg: O. Müller.

Kindermann, Heinz (1984): Das Theaterpublikum der Renaissance, Salzburg: O. Müller.

Klein, Robert / Zerner, Henri (1964): Vitruve et le théâtre de la Renaissance italienne, in: Jacquot (1964), pp. 49–60.

Koestermann, Erich (1932): Statio principis, Philologus 87, pp. 358–368; 430-444.

Kolb, Frank (2010): Augustus und das Rom aus Marmor — Glanz und Größe, in: Elke Stein-Hölkeskamp et al. (eds.): Erinnerungsorte der Antike: die römische Welt, Munich: Beck, pp. 123–39.

Kotte, Andreas (2013): Theatergeschichte, Cologne et al.: Böhlau.

Krause, Clemens (1985): Skenographie, Architektur und perspektivisches Sehen, in: Idem (ed.): La Prospettiva Pittorica, Geneva: Istituto Svizzero, pp. 43-77.

Krautheimer, Richard (1988): Scena tragica und Scena comica in der Renaissance – Die Tafeln in Baltimore und Urbino, in: id.: Ausgewählte Aufsätze zur europäischen Kunstgeschichte. Cologne: Dumont, pp. 334–356.

Lieberman, Ralph (2005): A scene from the life of Peruzzi, in: Anne B. Barriault et al. (eds.), Reading Vasari, London et. al.: Philip Wilson, pp. 147–53.

Little, Ian M.G. (1936): Scaenographia, in: The Art Bulletin 18, pp. 407–418.

Martines, Lauro (1963): The Social World of the Florentine Humanists, 1390–1460, Princeton: Princeton Univ. Press.

Marotti, Ferruccio (1974): Storia documentaria del teatro italiano. Lo spettacolo dall'Umanesimo al Manierismo. Teorica e tecnica. Milan: Feltrinelli.

Mohrmann, Christine (1953): Statio: Vigiliae christianae 7, pp. 221–245.

Molinari, Cesare (1964): Les rapports entre la scène et les spectateurs dans le theatre italien du XVI Siècle", in: Jacquot (1964), pp. 61–72.

Nagelsmit, Eelco (2002), Visualizing Vitruvius, in: Joost Keizer, Todd Richardson (eds): The Transformation of Vernacular Expression in Early Modern Arts, Leiden/Boston: Brill, pp. 339–72.

Nelis-Clément, Jocelyne (2006): Les stationes comme espace et transmission du pouvoir, in: Anne Kolb (ed.), Herrschaftsstrukturen und Herrschaftspraxis: Konzepte, Prinzipien und Strategien der Administration im römischen Kaiserreich, Berlin: De Gruyter, pp. 269–98.

France, Jérôme /Nelis-Clément, Jocelyne (2014): La statio. Archéologie d'un lieu de pouvoir dans l'empire romain, in: Jérôme France /Jocelyne Nelis-Clément (eds.): La statio. Archéologie d'un lieu de pouvoir dans l'empire romain, Bordeaux: Ausonius, pp. 11-17.

Ovid (1953): Tristia. Ex Ponto, Arthur L. Wheeler (ed., trans.), London/Cambridge MA: Harvard University Press.

Passow, Franz L. (1847): Handwörterbuch der griechischen Sprache, Leipzig: Vogel.

Payne, Alina (1999): The Architectural Treatise in the Renaissance: Architectural Invention, Ornament, and Literary Culture, Cambridge; Cambridge University Press.

Philandrier, Guillaume (2000): Les Annotations de Guillaume Philandrier sur le De architectura de Vitruve: livres I à IV. Repr. of the 1552 ed., Frédérique Lemerle (ed., trans., com.), Paris: Picard.

Pochat, Götz (1990): Theater und Bildende Kunst, Graz: Adeva.

Puttfarken, Thomas (2000): The Discovery of Pictorial Composition, New Haven/London: Yale University Press.

Puttfarken, Thomas (1994): Composition, Perspective and Presence. Observations on Early Academic Theory in France. In: John Onians (ed.). Sight and Insight. Essays on Art and Culture in Honour of E. H. Gombrich at 85, London: Phaidon Press, pp. 287-304.

Rivius (Ryff), Gualtherus Hermenius (1541): Des aller fürtrefflichsten, höchsten vnnd adelichsten gschöpffs aller Creaturen [...] Das ist des menschen [...] warfafftige beschreibung oder Anatomi, Straßburg: Beck.

Rivius (Ryff), Gualtherus Hermenius (1547): Der furnembsten, notwendigsten, der gantzen Architectur angehörigen Mathematischen und Mechanischen künst, eygentlicher bericht [...], Nürnberg: Petreius.

Rivius (Ryff), Gualtherus Hermenius (1548): Vitruvius Teutsch. Zehn Bücher von der Architectur und künstlichem Bauen, Nürnberg: Petreius.

Rivius (Ryff), Gualtherus Hermenius (ed.) (1543): M. Vitruvii, viri suae professionis peritissimi de Architectura libri decem [...] nunc primum in Germania [...] per Gualtherium H. Ryff. Argentinum, medicum, Strassbur: Egenolff.

Röttinger Heinrich (1914): Die Holzschnitte zur Architektur und zum Vitruvius Teutsch des Walther Rivius, Strasbourg: Heitz.

Roth, Simon (1571): Ein Teutscher Dictionarius / dz ist ein außleger schwerer/ vnbekanter Teutscher / Griechischer / Lateinischer / Hebraischer / Wẽlscher vnd Frantzẽsischer / auch andrer Nationen wẽrter [...], Augsburg: Manger, Michael.

Schalk, Fritz (1955): Das Publikum im italienischen Humanismus, Krefeld: Scherpe.

Schlikker, Friedrich Wilhelm (1940): Hellenistische Vorstellungen von der Schönheit des Bauwerks nach Vitruv, Berlin: Archäologisches Institut des Deutschen Reiches.

Schöne, Günter (1933): Die Entwicklung der Perspektivbühne von Serlio bis Galli-Bibiena nach den Perspektivbüchern. Leipzig: Voss.

Serlio, Sebastiano (1537): Regole generali di architettura di Sebastiano Serlio sopra le cinque maniere degli edifici, cioè, Thoscano, Dorico, Ionico, Corinthico, e composito con gliessempi de l'antiquita, Venice: Marcolino.

Serlio, Sebastiano (1540): Il terzo libro [...] nel qual si figurano; e descrivono le antiquità di Roma e le altre che sono in Italia, e fuori d'Italia, Venice: Marcolino.

Serlio, Sebastiano (1542a): Pieter Coecke van Aelst [and Jacob Rechlinger] (ed., trans.), Die gemaynen Reglen von der Architectur vber die funf Maniren, [Antwerp]: Couk.

Serlio, Sebastiano (1542b): Pieter Coecke van Aelst (ed., trans.), Reigles generales de l'Architecture, sur les cincq manieres [Antwerp]: Couk.

Serlio, Sebastiano (1545): Il primo libro d'Architettura, di Sebastiano Serlio, bolognese. Le premier livre d'Architecture de Sebastien Serlio, Bolognois, mis en langue Francoyse, par Ieahn Martin / Il secondo libro di perspettiva mis en langue Francoyse, par Ieahn Martin, Paris: Barbé.

Serlio, Sebastiano (1606): Den eersten vijfsten Boek van Architectural Sebastiani Serlii [...]. Overgeset uyt de Italiaensche in Nederduytsche sprake, door Pieter Coecke van Aelst, Amsterdam 1606.

Sebastiano Serlio (1609): Seb. Serlii Von der Architectur Fünff Bücher: Darinn die gantze lobliche und zierliche Bawkunst, sampt den Grundlegungen und Auffzügen manigerley Gebäuwen [...] gelehrt, und mit [...] Exemplen und Kunststucken [...] erklert wirdt [...], Basel: Ludwig König.

Serlio, Sebastiano (1611): The five Bookes of Architecture, made by Sebastian Serly ..., Robert Peake (ed., trans.), London: Printed for R. Peake.

Teeuwen, Stephan W. J. (1926): Sprachlicher Bedeutungswandel bei Tertullian: ein Beitrag zum Studium der christlichen Sondersprache, Paderborn: Schöningh.

Torello-Hill, Giulia (2014): The exegesis of Vitruvius and the creation of theatrical spaces in Renaissance Ferrara", in: Renaissance Studies 29/2, pp. 227–46.

Tybout, Rolf A. (1989): Die Perspektive bei Vitruv: Zwei Überlieferungen von scaenographia", in: Herman Geertman et. al. (eds.): Munus non ingratum, Proceedings of the International Symposium on Vitruvius' De Architectura and the Hellenistic and Republican Architecture, Leiden: Brill, pp. 55-68.

Vasari, Giorgio (1906): Le Vite de' più eccellenti pittori, scultori ed architettori [Florence, 1568], Gaetano Milanesi (ed.), Florence: Sansoni.

Vasari, Giorgio (1976): Le Vite de' più eccellenti pittori, scultori e architetti nelle redazioni del 1550 e 1568. Paola Barocchi and Rosanna Bettarini (eds.), Florence: Sansoni.

Vasari, Giorgio (1996): The Lives of the Painters. Sculptors and Architects, trans. Gaston du C. de Vere, 2 vols., New York: Alfred A. Knopf.

Vinci, Leonardo da (1882): Das Buch von der Malerei, Heinrich Ludwig (ed.), Vienna: Braumüller.

Vinci, Leonardo da (1883): Les manuscrits de Léonard de Vinci, les Manuscrits B & D de la Bibliothèque de l'Institut de France, M. Charles Ravaisson-Mollien (ed.), 6 vols., Paris: Quantin.

Vitruv (1976): De architectura libri decem = Zehn Bücher über Architektur, trans. and with a commentary by Curt Fensterbusch, Darmstadt: Wissenschaftliche Buchgesellschaft.

Vitruve (2009), Saliou, Catherine (ed., trans., com.), De l'architecture, livre V, Paris: CUF – Les Belles Lettres.

Vitruvius (1931): On Architecture, Frank Granger (ed., trans.), 2 vols., Cambridge/M: Harvard Univ. Press.

Vitruvius (1960 [1918]): The ten books on architecture, Morris Hicky Morgan (ed., trans.), London: Dover.

Watzinger Carl (1909): Vitruvstudien, in: Rheinisches Museum für Philologie, 64, pp. 202–23.

Wehnert, Martin (1966): Thema und Motiv, in: Musik in Geschichte und Gegenwart, Kassel: Bärenreiter.

Wellesz, Egon Joseph (1961): A History of Byzantine Music and Hymnography, Oxford: Clarendon Press.

Zanker, Paul (2003): Augustus und die Macht der Bilder, Munich: Beck.

Zedler, Johann Heinrich (1744): Stillstand der Planeten, in: Grosses Vollständiges Universal-Lexikon aller Wissenschaften und Künste, Leipzig/Halle: Johann Heinrich Zedler.

Figures

Fig. 1: *Engraving illustration by an unknown artist of the Terence comedies; edition Terentius: Comoediae, Strasbourg 1496*

Perspectival Stage and German Reception of *Second Book of Architecture* (1545) 77

Fig. 2a: Leonardo da Vinci, stage setting, Codex Atlanticus, fol. 358$^{v\text{-}b}$, Windsor 12,461 and 12,720, ca. 1485-95

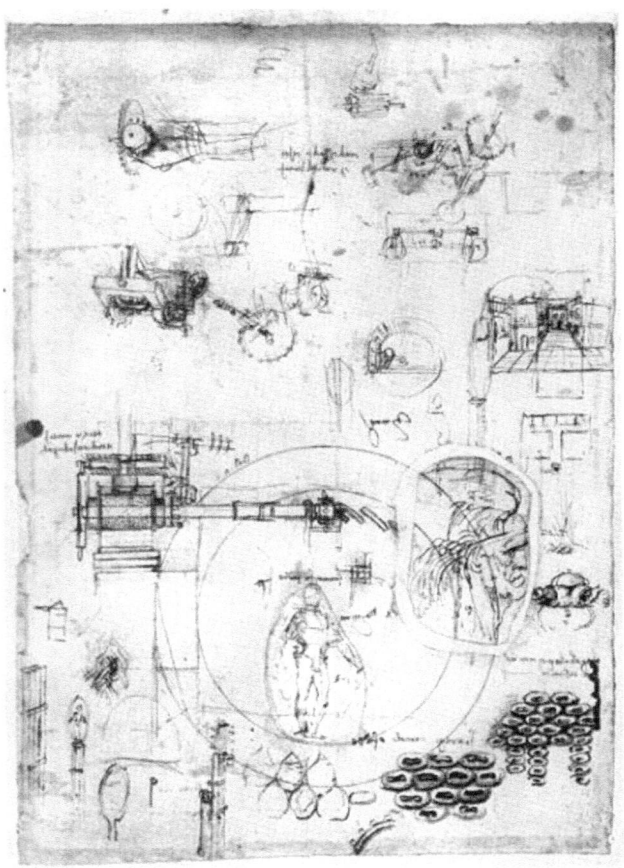

Fig. 2b: Leonardo da Vinci, stage setting, Codex Atlanticus, fol. 358^{v-b}, Windsor, ca. 1485-95

Fig. 3: Unknown Italian draftsman (formerly attributed to Baldassarre Peruzzi), perspective set with Roman buildings, mid sixteenth century (Gabinetto Disegni e Stampe, Uffizi Gallery, Florence UA291^r)

Fig. 4: After Bramante? Cesariano? A street with various buildings, colonnades and an arch. 1475?-1510? Engraving

Fig. 5: Sebastiano Serlio, Il secondo libro di perspettiva mis en langue Francoyse, par Ieahn Martin, Paris, 1545, ff. 35^v, 51^v

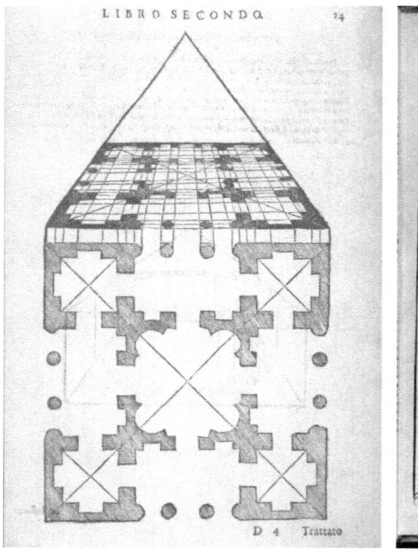

Perspectival Stage and German Reception of *Second Book of Architecture* (1545) 81

Fig. 6: Serlio, The Tragic Scene, Il secondo libro, fol. 69^v

Fig. 7: Ichnographia, orthographia, scaenographia, in Fra Giovanni Giocondo/Vitruvio, M. Vitruvius per Jocundum solito castigatior factus cum figuris et tabula… Venezia, G. da Tridentino, 1511, ff. 4 $^{r-v}$

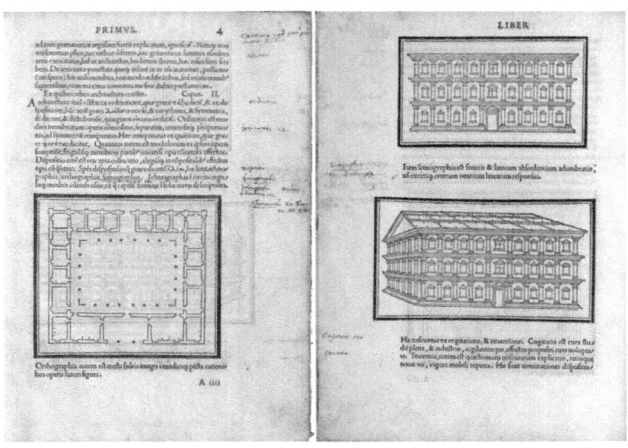

Fig. 8a: Periactoi in Iacomo Barozzi da Vignola / Ignazio Danti, Le due regole della prospettiva pratica, Bologna 1582, 91

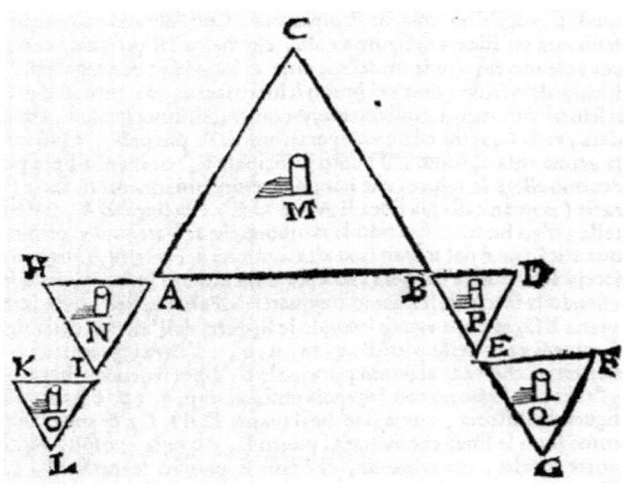

Fig. 8b: Joseph Furttenbach, Architectura Recreationis, Augsburg 1640, (134-35), Repr. Berlin 1988

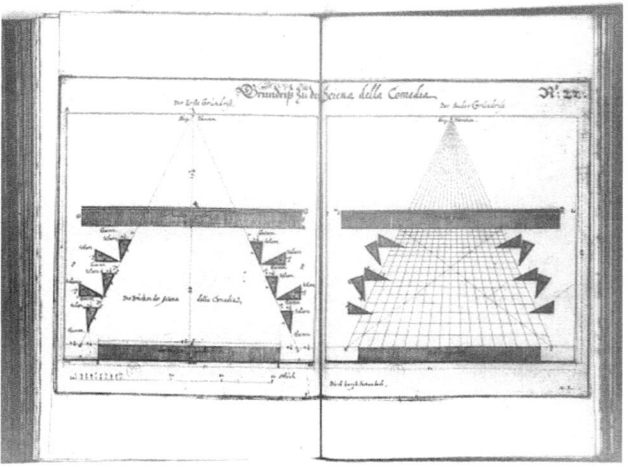

Fig. 9: Gualtherus Hermenius Rivius (Ryff), Vitruvius Teutsch. Zehn Bücher von der Architectur und künstlichem Bauen, Nürnberg 1548, fol. 177^v, 178^v, 179^r

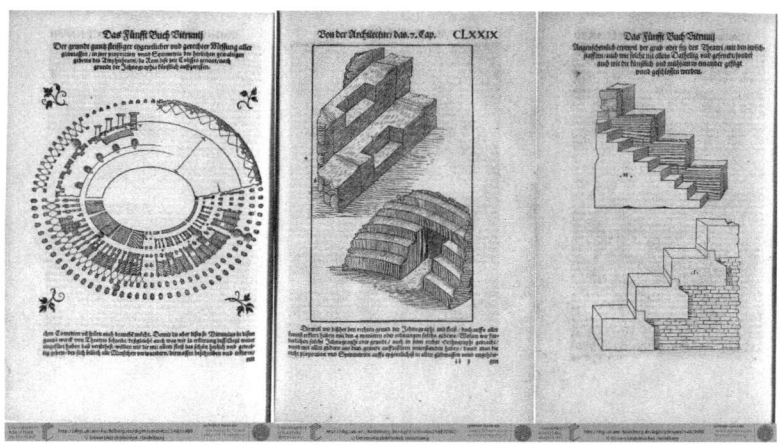

Fig. 10: Serlio, l terzo libro di Sebastiano Serlio Bolognese, nel qual si figurano: e descrivono le Antiquità, Venice 1540, ff. 64-65

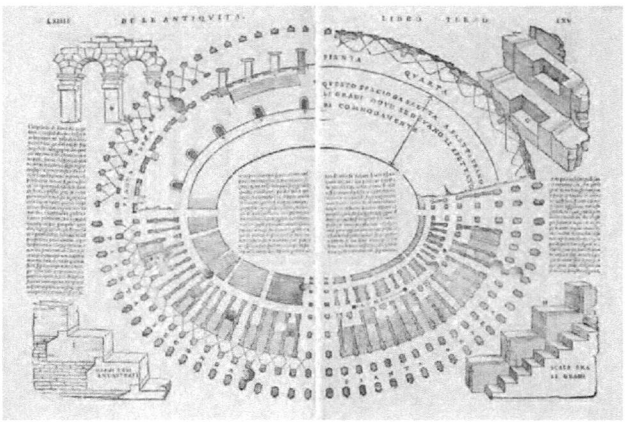

Fig. 11: Serlio, setting for comedy, in Secondo Libro, f. 71

Fig. 12: Leonardo da Vinci, "teatro da predicare", 1487-89 ca Paris, Institut de France, Ms. B, fol. 52ʳ

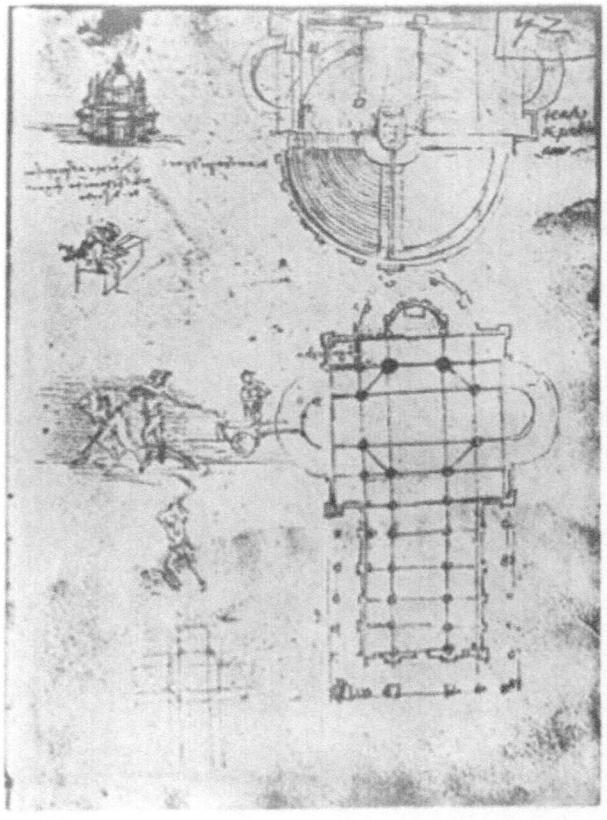

Fig. 13: Cesare Cesariano, Monopteral temple and architectural elements of the Roman theatre, engraving from a drawing from De Architectura libri dece traducti de latino in vulgare, Como 1521, fol. 81ᵛ

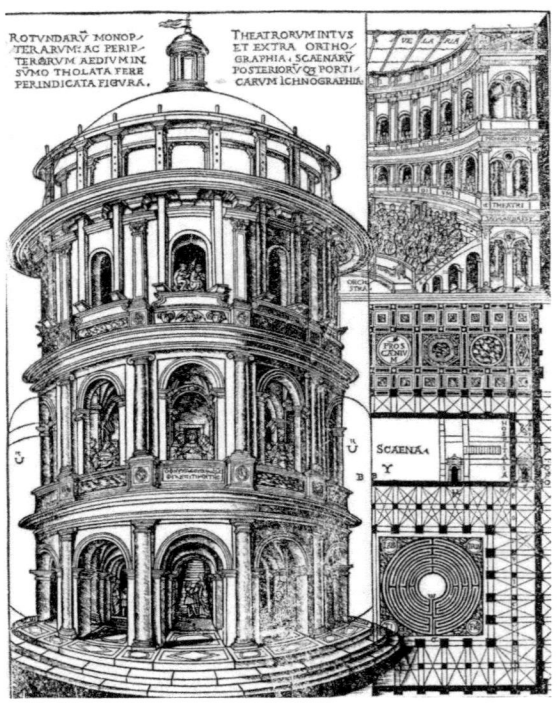

Fig. 14: The Theatre of Pompeius with temple of Venus Victrix, Rome, built around 55 BC according to the third century C.E. Severan marble plan (Forma Urbis Romae)

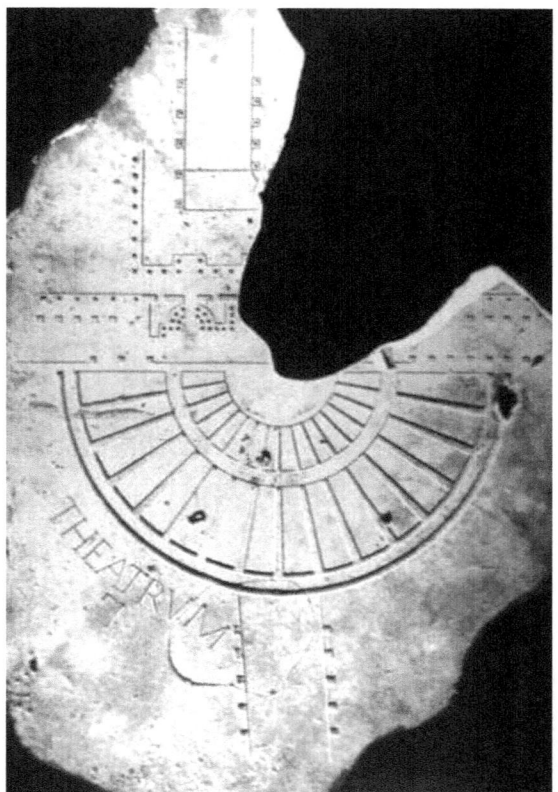

Fig. 15: Como Vitruvius, f. 75^v, 81^v; Ryff, Vitruvius Teutsch, f. 167^r

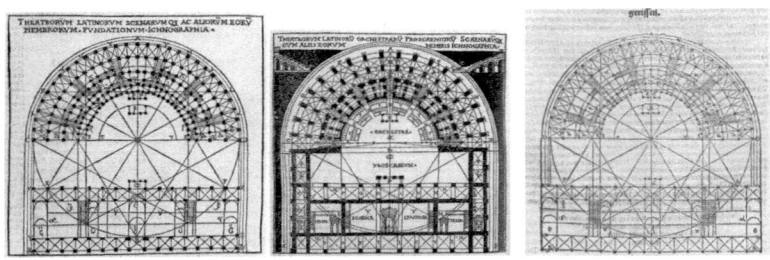

Fig. 16: Jan Stephan van Calcar: Frontispice from Andreas Vesalius, De humani corporis fabrica, Basel 1543

Perspectival Stage and German Reception of *Second Book of Architecture* (1545)   89

Fig. 17: Titus Maccius Plautus (c.254-184 BC), Comedies, edited by Bernard Saraceni, and Giovanni Pietro Valla. (Venice: Lazzaro de' Soardi) 1511

Central Perspective in Catholic Churches and on Stage in Europe between the 15th and 17th Centuries[1]

ISHIDA Yuichi

1.

The early 15th century produced the first painting in history to use geometric perspective. The fresco (circa 1425) of Masaccio (1401–1428), one of the leading painters of the Italian Renaissance, can be seen on the wall of the Church of Santa Maria Novella. It was based on a traditional image called *"Gnadenstuhl* (Throne of Grace)," depicting the Holy Trinity. Many art historians[2] have pointed out that this fresco belongs to the genealogy of so-called "visionary art," and according to George Bent, the Holy Trinity, together with the Virgin Mary and St. John the Evangelist, who also appear in the alcove, is nothing but a "vision" of the two kneeling and praying donors depicted in both lower corners of the fresco:

---

1   Part of this paper is an English translation of my previously published paper (Ishida 2019).
2   Paul Barolsky is one of the first to be considered an art historian. He stated, "[A]lthough the general tendency of Italian Renaissance art is toward the imitation of nature, the religious art of the period is primarily visionary [...]. This art illustrates or embodies visions, whether of images of saints gazing heavenward in ecstasy or heavenly buildings of remarkable luminosity and geometric perfection; it also encourages the worshiper to enter the spirit of the very vision that he beholds in illusion" (Barolsky 1995: 174). He deems the so-called "naturalism" of religious art since the mid-13th century as "a means by which the artist can bring the viewer into an immediate relationship with the supernatural or the sacred" and refers to Masaccio's fresco of the *Holy Trinity* as "a work which in the naturalistic power never ceases to hold us in thrall," as an example of such "visionary art" (Barolsky 1997: 57, 62).

> Their [the two kneeling donors'] inability to fix their gazes on the figures behind them suggests that the holy entourage is but a figment of their imagination, mystically produced because of proper devotional behavior. They enjoy a visionary experience invoked through prayer, which has in turn allowed them to imagine the broken body of the Savior. And we, in turn, have been granted access to their vision through the power of Masaccio's extraordinarily naturalistic rendering of it, as though the artist has informed us that if we adopt their pose and replicate their mental states, we too may experience this personal mystical revelation (Bent 2016: 274).

Masaccio created the impression by drawing a space with a vault ceiling strictly in accordance with the rules of geometric perspective in a semicircular arch painted on the wall so that, as Giorgio Vasari (1511–1574) said in the second edition of the *Lives* in 1567, "the wall appears to be pierced (*che pare che sia bucato quel muro*)" (Vasari 1966: III, 127). To see the space opened in the wall, it would simply not be enough to stand in front of the fresco; rather, beholders must also piously take an appropriate perspective, only from which can they see an alcove in the wall in which the Virgin and St. John will appear, pointing with hand or gaze to the Father supporting the cross from behind, the Son on the cross, and the Holy Spirit in the form of a white dove spreading its wings. Indeed, according to Paul Barolsky, it is exactly this "pictorial 'vision' of the Trinity" that "all who beheld the fresco were intended to experience":

> We dwell on the perspective, modeling, and sculptural relief of the fresco, but to what end are these elements of art articulated? We are so overwhelmed by Masaccio's naturalism, and understandably so, that we rarely draw the obvious conclusion from a scrutiny of his fresco's eternal mystery that, in rendering the illusion of the presence of such a mystery, the painter's naturalism brings to the worshiper's mundane eyes an elevated, transcendental subject, which he thus sees as in a vision. Masaccio's naturalism serves his visionary purpose of affording the viewer an initial stage in the vision of the mystery of the trinity as if beheld in the church itself. (Barolsky 1997: 63)

In the mysticism of the late Middle Ages, devotions emphasizing visionary experiences in meditation and contemplation held a certain position. A manuscript of a treatise for nuns, *Livres de l'estat de l'ame* (*Books on the States of the Soul*), produced at the end of the 13th century, has a miniature illustrating such devotional work in four scenes. The first scene shows a nun confessing to a monk and a speech scroll held by an angel says, "If you want to erase your sins, say, 'Have mercy'" (*Si uis delere tua crimina dic miserere*). In the second scene, the nun is praying in front of the statue of the *Coronation of the Virgin*. In the third, a vision of Christ emerges from a circle of clouds, telling the prostrating nun, "See how much I bore for the life of the people!" (*pro vita populi respice quanta tuli*). In the final scene, the vision of the Holy Trinity appears in the circle of clouds, and the speech scroll says, "The Father, the Word, and the Holy Spirit, these three are one" (*Pater uerbum spiritus sanctus hii tres unum sunt*)—so the mystery of the Holy Trinity is revealed to the nun kneeling and staring at the vision. (Brantley 2007: 325; Belting 2011: 459–60; Falque 2019: 203–204)

This last stage, at which mystical devotions aim, is nothing less than what Masaccio painted on the wall of the Church of Santa Maria Novella. Just as the nun saw the vision of the Holy Trinity in the last scene of the miniature, the two donors see it in Masaccio's fresco. Furthermore, this fresco, by using perspective, enables the vision that the donors in the painting are having to also be seen by the eyes of those who pray in front of the fresco. In other words, perspective was a technique to make those who gazed piously on religious paintings artificially experience visions that revealed the mysteries of the Christian faith to them.

2.

While the visionary experience had gained some position in the mystical devotions of the Middle Ages, according to art historian Kikuro Miyashita it was often perceived as dangerous by church authorities, and more than a few alleged seers of visions were executed for the sin of heresy. This was because visionary experiences established a direct relationship between an individual and God without church mediation. In the 16th century, the process of personalization and internalization of faith had already gone so far as to be undeniable, prompting the Catholic Church to treat it as a way to oppose the biblicism of the Protestant Church. Hence, the visionary experiences of saints such as St. Ignatius of Loyola and St. Teresa of Avila, who led the Catholic Reformation, were actively proclaimed as "hallmarks of the saints" and were painted in many pictures (Miyashita 2004: 119–120). For example, St. Ignatius, founder of the Jesuits, while praying at a chapel in the village of La Storta on his way to Rome, experienced a vision of God the Father and Christ holding the cross, and he heard Christ saying, "My desire is that you will be my servant," with the Father saying, "I shall be propitious to you in Rome." According to William Bangert,

> This vision left Ignatius with an increased desire that his little band be known as the Society of Jesus and with a deeper confidence in God's protection regardless of what Rome might have in store for them (Bangert 1972: 19).

This visionary experience was handed down as the founding myth of the Jesuits, and many painters portrayed saints kneeling and praying, looking at the vision of the Father and Christ.

The saints wrote down their visionary experiences in their diaries and letters, which made their way into the saints' respective biographies, but of course, none could share or experience for him- or herself such personal and internal occurrences as visions—at any rate, by means of narratives; even if visualized in a painting, the vision could never be experienced by viewers as their own, so long as it was depicted beside or above the saint who saw it, as is the case in many visionary paintings of early modern times.

However, in the 17th century, as the ceilings of churches were increasingly adorned with frescoes in perspective, those who looked upward in churches came to experience the saints' vision themselves (Miyashita 2004: 120–121). For example, if one stands at a point marked with yellow marble on the floor in the nave of the Church of Sant'Ignazio in Rome and look up, they will see that the church's real walls and pillars do not end where they reach the ceiling but continue further into the open sky that was filled with angels and various anthropomorphic figures. Then, at the vanishing point just above the position of the viewer, St. Ignatius' vision at La Storta—the Father and Christ holding the cross—emerges as an image of the Holy Trinity, with a dove representing the Holy Spirit. In addition, St. Ignatius, who should be seeing this vision, also enters the vision itself, spreading his hands toward Christ, floating in the heavens, and catching the light emitted from Christ on his chest (Miyashita 2004: 121). From there, the light is reflected in all directions and reaches Europe, Asia, Africa, and America (Bangert 1972: 190; Japanese translation: upper, 365–366). E. H. Gombrich writes of this magnificent ceiling fresco, created by painter and architect Andrea Pozzo (1642–1709), a Jesuit lay brother:

> To call such a composition, with all its attendant symbolic beings and signs, illusionistic seems to me again to be straining the meaning of the word; but we may call it an evocation which turns us into visionary eyewitnesses of

that mystery which the Church desires to convey to the faithful (Gombrich 1999: 43).

This "mystery," which is no less than the one that St. Ignatius was called by Christ at La Storta to spread to the whole world, emerges in the eyes of the faithful viewers of the ceiling fresco as the rays emitted from Christ, reflecting off the chest of St. Ignatius and radiated in all directions, so that the viewers literally become "visionary eyewitnesses of that mystery."

The ceiling frescoes adorning the interiors of Catholic churches are often viewed as the opposite of the internalized spirituality of the Protestant faith. However, it is not just a superficial decoration but rather, as Gombrich says, "an evocation which turns us into visionary eyewitnesses of that mystery which the Church desires to convey to the faithful," so the mysteries and miracles can be experienced in an internalized way called "a vision." In this regard, the following passage, described by Erwin Panofsky in the last paragraph of *Perspective as Symbolic Form*, is suggestive:

> Perspective...pens it [religious art] to something entirely new, the realm of the visionary, where the miraculous becomes a direct experience of the beholder, in that the supernatural events in a sense erupt into his own, apparently natural, visual space and so permit him really to "internalize" their supernaturalness (Panofsky 1991: 72).

Miracles were once thought to take place in the public eye, with eyewitnesses, but since the 16th century, as religion became more and more individualized and internalized, miracles became an internal phenomenon that can be experienced in such personal ways as visions. In such an era, perspective was a means of opening "the realm of the visionary" where the miracles could be, as Panovsky says, "a direct experience of the beholder," which was opened not simply to a chosen few such as saints, but also to all faithful people.

3.

Today, however, anyone who steps into Pozzo's church should have the following doubts, as expressed by French writer Dominique Fernandez in his book *Le Banquet des Anges (The Feast of Angels)*:

> As we go deep into the church, we may even ask ourselves: are we really in the church? Wasn't it rather to a theater that Pozzo invited us?...Would the

Catholic religion be just an illusion? Wouldn't the altar on which the divine sacrifice is performed have more consistency than an opera set? (Fernandez 1984: 77–80).

In the late 17th century, during Pozzo's time, as Fernandez put it, "Opera, a play of mirrors of all illusions, has definitively established itself as the first of the arts" (Fernandez 1984: 83). By Pozzo's birth in 1642, several public theaters had already stood in Venice, and the era of the public opera house had begun. In particular, the perspective stage of the Novissimo Theater was completed by Giacomo Torelli in 1641 and was used to instantaneously change the scenes, earning a great reputation (Visentin 2019: 391–392). Not surprisingly, on a stage where opera was performed, perspective was not intended to give the viewer a glimpse of the mystery of the church, but rather to create what Corneille called "*illusion comique* (theatrical illusion)." This being so, we cannot help supposing that Pozzo, who lived in such an era, looked at the interior of the cathedral he worked on and doubted himself, asking, "Would the Catholic religion be just an illusion?"

These suspicions deepen as Pozzo refers to his scenery or settings with which he decorated the high altar of churches during the Forty Hours' Devotion service with the term *theatrum* in his own book, *Perspectiva Pictorum et Architectorum* (Rome 1693–1702). Because it was a temporary setting that was removed at the end of the ceremony, no genuine example of it can be seen today. However, Pozzo's book includes ground plans, single-view drawings, and perspective drawings of such settings, the most famous example of which was one made for the ceremony at the Gesù Church in Rome in 1685. According to Pozzo's own commentary, this setting was perspectively constructed to visualize Jesus' miracle of turning water into wine at a wedding feast in the town of Cana in Galilee. It is noteworthy that Pozzo calls it *"Theatrum repraesentans nuptias Cana Galileae* (*theatrum* that represents the wedding at Cana in Galilee)" (Pozzo 1706: Fig. 71) and that he also writes: *"Theatris quae jam delineavimus affinia sunt theatra scenica"* (the *Theatra*, which have been illustrated so far, is similar to theatrical *theatra*") (Pozzo 1706: Fig. 72). "*Theatris quae jam delineavimus affinia*" refers to the perspective settings that Pozzo created for church ceremonies, including the one in 1685, whereas "*theatra scenica*" means stages for theater performance as we know them today. In other words, Pozzo points out similarities between settings for altar decoration and those for theater stages, and some illustrations in his book showing the mechanism of his altar decoration clearly show that it is a double of the stage settings that were designed and constructed for baroque theaters.

Fig. 1: *Theatrum sacrum (Fig. 71) erected in 1685 in the Jesuit church in Rome and representing the Marriage at Cana in Pozzo's Perspectivo Pictorum et Architectorum, Rome, 1693–1702*

If so, it must be said that Fernandez's statement that Pozzo "turned the church's most sacred place into a theater" (Fernandez 1984: 80; 70) would be justified. It should be noted, however, that Pozzo does not claim that his settings for altar decoration are similar to those for the theater stage, but rather that the latter are similar to the former, and that the term *"theatrum"* did not necessarily imply facilities for theater performances in the 17th century (Fischer-Lichte 1997: 12). In the classical Roman era, the term certainly indicated a building with an area where actors perform and a semicircular auditorium, but since the Middle Ages, such buildings have fallen into ruins and been forgotten and, as a result, *"theatrum"* has lost its classical meaning and been used instead in its broadest sense as simply a "place for seeing" (Marshall 1950: 382). The classical meaning of the word was revived in the *Ten Books on Architecture* (*De Architectura*), written by ancient Roman architect Vitruvius (ca. 40 BC), "rediscovered" ca. 1414 CE, first edited by Giovanni Sulpicio of Veroli, and probably published in Rome in 1486. Its first illustrated edition edited by Fra Giocondo was published in Venice in 1511. However, as we can see from the term *"theatrum anatomicum,"* which meant a hall used for anatomical lectures and demonstrations, the term *"theatrum"* was not limited to facilities for theatrical or dramatic performance but also had a more general meaning of "place for seeing," and its meaning was restricted only by adding adjectives (Anderson 1991: 7). Pozzo's use of *"theatrum"* in this broad sense can also be seen from the fact that he refers to the stage setting for theater performance with such compound terms as *"theatrum scenicum"* (*"scenicum"* means "theatrical" or "belonging to the stage") or *"theatrum comicum"* (Pozzo 1706: Fig. 72, Pozzo1719: Figs. 37, xx), whereas he calls his altar decoration for church ceremonies *"theatrum sacrum"* (Pozzo 1719: Fig. 45). For him, the former is not at all the original meaning of the word "theatrum"; it is just one example of it. It would be no surprise, then, that Pozzo used the term "theatrum" to describe his scenery for altar decoration in church. His use of this term is not a metaphorical one that compares an altar to a theater. Rather, "theatrum sacrum" is a "place for seeing" the mysteries and miracles of God, and in this literal sense, it was worthy of being called a *theatrum*.

On the other hand, probably from the late 17th century, the visual space created by perspective underwent a significant change in its cultural connotation. With the rise of opera in the mid-17th century and the spread of perspective stage settings in public theaters, perspective itself became increasingly suggestive of theatrical illusionism, which was mainly aimed to provide spectators with visual amusement and distraction, and along with it, even churches' ceiling and walls that were painted in perspective came to be perceived as being similar to a backdrop for theater performances, and consequently perspective lost religious significance. It was just this new perception that was, and is still today, repeatedly articulated by many critics and writers such as Fernandez. At the end of the 17th century, however, the faithful Jesuit lay brother Pozzo seems apparently to have been not seriously aware of this change yet, otherwise he could not so innocently have designed *"theatrum sacrum"* for church ceremonies on one hand, *"theatrum scenicum"* or *"theatrum comicum"* for such performances as "Jesuit school theater" on the other hand.[3]

Of course, the interior space of churches did not abruptly cease to be decorated with perspective frescoes; even in the so-called Rococo era, the ceilings of many churches were, as formerly, adorned with such paintings, and even in the second half of the 18th century, the practice of decorating altars with perspective scenery for the Sunday of the Resurrection continued not only in the city's cathedrals but also in small churches and monasteries in rural areas such as Silesia and the Tyrol region. However, in 1782, such altar decorations for church ceremonies were banned by Holy Roman Emperor Joseph II (1741–1790) (Grass 1957; Töpler 1998). They were, in the eyes of the enlightened despot of the 18th century, no longer what Gombrich calls "an evocation which turns us into visionary eyewitnesses of that mystery which the Church desires to convey to the faithful," but rather theater settings that can only create empty illusions. This means that the curtain of the Baroque age has been closed, and that imaginary space that Panofsky calls the "realm of the visionary" has also been completely closed against "religious art." If this "realm" once opened by perspective was the last space where "the miraculous" could—albeit only

---

3   Cp. Kemp 1987: 263. "Pozzo's use of illusion can be aligned with a range of images which use perspective and related optical techniques as a form of natural magic to evoke awe in the spectator. [...] A series of optical curiosities, including the magic lantern, came to serve the dual ends of entertainment and spiritual expression. The great German Jesuit philosopher in Rome around the middle of the century, Athanasius Kircher, perfectly expresses the extraordinary compound of scientific acumen, natural magic, astrological mysticism, Neoplatonic rapture and Cristian fervour which lies behind the ambitions of Pozzo and his patrons. It was in this context that sacred art could become a form of theater, expressing through illusion those spiritual truths whose presence on earth was manifested only through elusive reflections and shadows. Pozzo's placing of illusion in the service of mystical ends should not be taken to imply that he regarded the optical means as anything other than a wholly rational system which corresponded in a direct way to the physical-cum-mathematical basis of vision."

in completely "internalized" ways—be experienced, then after the complete closure of this space it is only natural that "the Life of Jesus" without mysteries and miracles would be told openly by such 19th-century writers as David Friedrich Strauss (1808–1874) and Ernest Renan (1823–1892).

References

Anderson, Michael (1991): "The Changing Scene: Plays and Playhouses in the Italian Renaissance." In: J.R. Mulryne/Margaret Shrewring (eds.), Theatre of the English and Italian Renaissance, New York: St. Martin's Press , pp. 3-20.

Bangert, William V. (1972): A History of the Society of Jesus, 2th ed., St. Louis: The Institute of Jesuits Sources.

Barolsky, Paul (1995): "The visionary experience of Renaissance Art." In: Word and Image 11, pp. 174-181.

Barolsky, Paul (1997): "Naturalism and the Visionary Art of the Early Renaissance." In: Gazette des Beaux-Arts 129, pp. 57-64.

Belting, Hans (2011): Bild und Kult—Eine Geschichte des Bildes vor dem Zeitalter der Kunst, 7th ed., Munich: Beck.

Bent, George (2016): Public Painting and Visual Culture in Early Republican Florence, New York: Cambridge University Press.

Brantley, Jessica (2007): "Vision, Image, Text." In: Paul Strohm (ed.), Middle English: Oxford Twenty-First Century Approaches to Literature, Oxford: Oxford University Press, pp.315-334.

Falque, Ingrid (2019): Devotional Portraiture and Spiritual Experience in Early Netherlandish Painting, Leiden/London: Brill.

Fischer-Lichte, Erika (1997): The Show and the Gaze of Theatre: A European Perspective, Iowa City, IA: University Iowa Press.

Fernandez, Dominique (1984): Le Banquet des Anges: L'Europe baroque de Rome à Praque, Paris: Pion.

Gombrich, E. H. (1999): "Painting on Walls: Means and Ends in the History of Fresco Painting." In: The Uses of Images: Studies in the Social Function of Art and Visual Communication, pp.14-47, London: Phaidon Press, pp. 14-47.

Grass, Nikolaus (1957) "Barock-Heiliggräber: Ein Beitrag zur Kultur- und Kunstgeschichte Tirols." In: Nikolaus Grass/Emil Berlanda/Georg Schreiber (eds.), Ostern in Tirol, Innsbruck: Wagner, pp. 221–269.

Kemp, Martin (1987): "Perspektive and Meaning: Illusion, Allusion, and Collusion." In: Andrew Harrison (ed.), Philosophy and the Visual Arts: Seeing and Abstracting. Dordrecht: D. Reidel Publishing Company, pp. 255-268.

Ishida, Yuichi (2019): "Shimpi no genshiteki taiken shudan to shite no enkinhô: Kinsei no kyôkai kenchiku ni okeru enkinhôteki iryûjonizumu no imi to kinô." In: Doitsu bunka 74, pp. 43-63.

Marshall, Mary H. (1950): "Theatre in the Middle Ages: Evidence from Dictionaries and Glosses." In Symposium: A Quarterly Journal in Modern Literatures 4/1, pp. 1–39.

Miyashita, Kikuro. 2004. Karavajjo: Seisei to vijon. Nagoya: Nagoya daigaku shuppankai.

Panofsky, Ervin (1991): Perspective as Symbolic Form. New York: Zone Books.

Pozzo, Andrea (1693): Perspectiva Pictorum et Architectorum Andreae Putei [...], Rome: Komarek

Pozzo, Andrea (1706): Perspectivae Pictorum Atque Architectorium / Der Mahler und Baumeister Perspectiv [...], Augsburg: Jeremias Wolff.

Shimbo, Kiyono (2000): "Kuarantôre shukusai sôchi no bunseki: Taikôshûkyôkaikakuki Rôma no Iezusukai fuzoku shintokai shusai shukusai." In: Bijutsushi 50/1, pp. 79-96.

Töpler, Winfried (1998): "Das Heilige Grab von Neuzelle." In: Walter Ederer/Klaus Reinecke (eds.) Sein grab wird Herrlich seijn. Das Heilige Grab von Neuzelle und seine Passionsdarstellungen von 1751, Regensburg: Schnell & Steiner, pp. 17-51.

Vasari, Giorgio (1966): Le Vite de' più eccellenti pittori, scultori e architetti nelle redazioni del 1550 e 1568. Ed. and with a commentary by Paola Barocchi and Rosanna Bettarini, 6 vols, Florence: Sansoni.

Visentin, Hélène (2019): "Machinery Plays." In: John D. Lyons (ed.) *The Oxford Handbook of the Baroque*, New York: Oxford University Press, pp. 386-408.

Notable Spectacles in the Late 19th-Century Kabuki Stage

HIOKI Takayuki

During the late Tokugawa period and the Meiji era, which is about the second half of the 19th century in the Christian era, Kabuki direction using props and gunpowder was prominent. I aim to examine the actual situation of these directions.

In Edo Kabuki during the late 18th century to the early 19th century, the popularity of flashy directions using prop gimmicks has often been pointed out. In particular, TSURUYA Namboku IV has written many works that used such effects. Namboku's works used the so-called spectacle to show the superhuman abilities of entities such as ghosts and sorcerers. The direction in *toita-gaeshi*—in which one actor, in quick changes, plays the ghosts of a man and a woman crucified on both sides of a single-door panel, devised at the premiere of the masterpiece *Tôkaidô Yotsuya kaidan*—and in *chôchin-nuke*, in which a ghost appears from a burning lantern, added in a replay of the same work, is well-known and still used today with refinement.

ICHIKAWA Kodanji IV is one of the actors who played an active role in the latter half of the 19th century while inheriting the abovementioned directions from ONOE Kikugorô III, who appeared in Namboku's works and in many ghost stories, and from HASEGAWA Kambei XI, a stagehand. I abstracted stage directions that seem to have used the gimmick from Kodanji's work:

> With usu-dorodoro [weird drum sounds], from under the armrest that Hikosaburô [disguised as Masatomo] leans on, Kodanji appears as a ghost of Tôgo and looks up at Hikosaburô's face from below.

Looking at Imba. Ô-dorodoro [violent drum sounds]. Imba changes into the appearance of the ghost of Tôgo played by Kodanji, and because it looks reproachful [...][1]

[...] usu-dorodoro, netori [weird flute sounds], hitotsu-gane [a bell sound], fire on alcohol burns with uncanny music, and from the stage left an artificial corpse which is covered with woven straw, and on which a wild goose puppet perches, comes into the center. [. . .] The wild goose mentioned above flies away. The corpse gradually gets up, and the woven straw mat falls, then Kodanji, who plays two roles [in this piece], opens his eyes possessing the body of Koheiji and he goes immediately up to the stage with a gimmick. He tries to enter inside, scared by a paper charm [. . .] The body of Kodanji [Koheiji's ghost] enter in front of the lattice with a gimmick. After dorodoro, Shimazô [a servant woman] gets up with the sound of waves, looks at the trace.

Sanjûrô puts a sake bottle into a steel bottle to warm the sake, and drinks it. Dorodoro, netori, hitotsugane, uncanny music, Kodanji as Koheiji appears from the edge of mosquito net and advances to a suitable spot.

With dorodoro, netori, and uncanny music, Kodanji appears as Koheiji from the yukata [casual kimono] put by [Otsuka, played by] IMAI Kumesaburô, and advances to a suitable spot.[2]

Here, the ghosts appear and disappear from objects such as the armrest, the yukata clothes, and mosquito nets. Also portrayed are the appearance of other people instantly turning into the shape of ghosts, their strange way of walking, and others. Many of the techniques used for such directions are unknown in detail, but some of them are illustrated in Edo period drama books such as *Shibai kinmô zui* (1803), and some have been inherited by the current stage.

Furthermore, from the late Edo period to the Meiji era, with the development of prop gimmicks, theatrical performances depicting events different

---

1 "Higashiyama sakura zôshi" (1851). Cited and translated from Kokuritsu gekijô chôsa yôseibu 2015: 272-273.

2 "Kohada-no kaii ame-no furunuma" (1860). Cited and translated from Kokuritsu gekijô chôsa yôseibu 2013: 233-235.

from those involving ghosts and monsters—disasters and wars—have become prominent.[3]

Also, in reality, the late 19th century was a period of frequent disasters in Japan. Buildings of the Edo period heavily used wood, which meant large-scale fires often occurred in large cities such as Edo. In addition, in 1854, the Ansei Tôkai Earthquake and the Ansei Nankai Earthquake, both estimated at M8.4, occurred in rapid succession, and a large earthquake directly underneath Edo struck the following year.

On the other hand, the Edo era was a peaceful time in which no significant civil wars as well as foreign wars took place after the Shimabara Rebellion from 1637 to 1638, but from 1868 to 1869, after the Boshin War, when government troops fought against the former Shogunate forces, rebels broke out everywhere and continued until the Meiji period. The last but largest one was the 1877 Satsuma Rebellion. Japan in the Meiji period would also experience the First Sino–Japanese War of 1894–1895, the Russo–Japanese War of 1904–1905, and wars with other foreign countries.

At least until the Sino–Japanese War, drama in Japan still maintained its role as news media. At a time when movie did not exist, it was of great value to show the damaged areas and battlefields in motion, which could not be seen by people in real time.

At the end of the Tokugawa period, despite the fictional narrative of works such as *Takagi Oriemon budô jitsuroku* (1848) and *Tsukimi-no hare meiga-no ichijiku* (1862), one can see scenes of flashy underwater movements. As an example, let us examine the designation of props for flood scenes, which was set up in the finale of *Ichibannori meiki-no sashimono*, which was staged in 1865:

> The backcloth in the middle part of the stage is turned back and becomes silver waves. A three-tiered *jigasuri* [cloth that cover the stage to express the ground] is turned back, undulated and also becomes silver waves. The first fence painted waves is pushed out to the pillar on the right stage and fill the perpendicular direction. The second and third fences are also pushed out successively at the good timing and the boxes on both sides are undulated. The entire flat stage is covered with waves, and finally it begins to rain: the whole is the representation of a flood. (Kawatake (n. d.))

The spectacle of the flood was represented by a backcloth that drew waves as well as wave cloths ranging not only from the stage but also to the boxes, that

---

3 For disasters and wars in the Kabuki theatre of the time, see Hioki 2016: 101-164.

is, the audience seats. And on the stage, three partitions called wave-fences (*nami-tesuri*) were installed, which also generated waves, and the actors came and went in the waves and performed various acts.

In the Meiji era, more realistic effects were performed. For example, *Torioi Omatsu kaishô banashi*, which was performed for the first time in 1879, features a scene in which a heroine falls from a cliff to rough seas and is saved by a steamboat, and when *Hyôryû kidan seiyô kabuki* was performed, a new method for drawing scenes on the sea was created by HASEGAWA Kambei XIV, a stagehand. Kambei was dissatisfied with the production of the traditional scenes on the sea.

> In the previous plays, when they showed scenes on the sea, they only placed wave panels on the stage and used wave cloth in the background, which were very simple props. Now, when he shows scenes of wrecks on the sea, he can never use such old props that do not move, so the perfectionist Kambei has eagerly thought of somehow showing how real waves move.[4]

Holding such thoughts, Kambei rode a ferry across the Sumida River in a storm. While observing the surface of the water, he came up with a new trick using props.

> The wave cloth is stretched all over the stage, and two-inch square sticks are erected in some places under it to create a free space. Some people hide beneath the cloth and kick it, and then, it looks like the real waves are rising. The spring of a rickshaw is attached to the back of the ship, and it passes through the road between the waves, so it sways as if it were drifting in the waves due to the spring mechanism.[5]

Two years later, in *Shima-chidori tsuki no shiranami*, which premiered at the same Shintomi-za theatre, one can see a scene where the protagonist, Akashi no Shimazô, rows in rough seas, and here, the new technology in *Hyôryû kidan seiyô kabuki* was likely reused.

Sampu goko utsusu gentô, also staged in 1887 in Shintomi-za theatre, is based on the Normanton case in which a British-registered cargo ship, the Normanton, wrecked and killed all its Japanese passengers, and it was later found that it was impossible to hold its British captain criminally liable for abandoning the passengers because of the unequal treaty between Britain and

---

4 "Shogei ichiryû ima no meijin." In: Yomiuri Shimbun, October 21, 1903.
5 Ibid.

Japan at that time. In a picture on the program, one can see the words "A Great Spectacle of Steamship Sinking!," indicating that it was one of the highlight scenes. According to KIMURA Kinka, a playwright and producer, the magician KITENSAI Shôichi showed the moon using a magic lantern and ignited magnesium to express lightning. Kimura said, "The scene showing a terrible wreck of a large ship presented as a stage set being swallowed by heavy waves and sinking was realistic and earned applause" (Kimura1943: 764-5).

The technology used to depict floods and shipwrecks in a fictional world has become increasingly sophisticated and has been used to portray real-world accidents. Many plays based on the Meiji Sanriku Earthquake Tsunami in 1896 may have been performed using such techniques. The tsunami that struck on June 15 of the same year has been staged in theaters around the country since early July 1896. Although it is not Kabuki but rather a play of the new school, *Ô-tsunami*, played by the Ii Yôhô Company in Asakusa-za theatre in Tokyo, and the play that had the same title by FUKUI Mohei in Kyoto-za incorporates an event reported in newspapers in which SATÔ Jin, an elementary school teacher at Okirai Village (now Ôfunato City) in Iwate Prefecture, rescued an imperial portrait enshrined inside the school, heedless of danger. The program in Miyako-za theatre shows a man with the imperial portrait braving through the waves, and this scene may have also been performed using wave cloths, as described above.

Also, fires and other disasters were actively depicted on stage during the Meiji era, and war cannot be overlooked in terms of reflecting actual events. As mentioned earlier, the Meiji era began with the civil war and was an era of many wars, including foreign ones, which Kabuki also depicted.

Hazama gunki Narumi no kikigaki, performed at Morita-za in 1870, and *Meiji nenkan azuma nikki*, performed at Shintomi-za in 1875, depict the Ueno War in May 1868, a battle that took place in Ueno, near the city area of Edo. It is recorded that the use of gunpowder attracted the audience's interests; the battle scene of *Okige no kumo harau asagochi* at Shintomi-za in 1878 depicted the Satsuma Rebellion, a civil war that broke out the previous year: "The scene with a hail of bullets looked realistic, and the use of Western-style fireworks at the scene of death and falling from a horse in battle surprised the audiences because such fireworks were rare at that time" (Tamura 1976 [1922]: 206).

During the First Sino–Japanese War and the Russo–Japanese War, plays depicted the battles between warships. Act IV of *Nippon daishôri* of Haruki-za in September 1894, which was performed during the Sino–Japanese War, showed Qing (China) warships being sunk by the Japanese navy and soldiers jumping off into the sea, performed as follows: "The cannons roar and shoot from the warships of Japan. They hit on the [warship] Kôraku, and the Kôraku breaks off and gradually sinks. The smoke fireworks burn and Qing soldiers cry, wander, and finally jump into the wave cloths."[6] There was also the scene of a naval battle in *Aizu-san Meiji no kumijû*, which was staged at the Meiji-za theatre in October. The script says,

> Their lines stop, and they hit a beat. Then, the center of the Qing warship is broken by the gimmick, fireworks sound, a fire breaks out from inside the warship, the fire rises here and there in black smoke, and the ship gradually sinks. The rifles sound often, the ship sinks into the sea, and there is left only its mast. The sound of wind is strong, and the Qing flag is cut, flies by the strings, turns round and round, and is drawn up to the upper stage; meanwhile, the mast gradually goes into the sea. (Kawatake 1929: 687-8)

As seen above, the production, including its mechanisms, is described in detail.

Also, in the Russo–Japanese War from 1904 to 1905, the sinking of the Russian fleet was set as a stage. Engeki-za's *Ryojun-kô heisoku* depicts the Port Arthur Blockade Operation, in which Lieutenant Colonel HIROSE Takeo famously died. The following description of the scene is interesting:

> In the last piece, *Ryojun-kô heisoku*, the gimmick is used to show the sinking of the Normanton in Shintomi-za last year. When the hull sinks underwater, an officer on the mast, commanding, takes down the boat, jumps on it, and rows offshore. Meanwhile, the officer is represented by a child actor and then by a puppet [the officer looks smaller and smaller, and the impression that the boat is receding into the distance is created], and the scene moves naturally. The gimmick is like a movie.[7]

The direction of the *Normanton* sinking in Shintomi-za was diverted to the sinking of the Russian warship. When they depicted the officers who fled to sea by boat and went offshore by emphasizing perspective using child actors and dolls, "wave-fences," as seen on the stage set of *Ichibannori meiki-no sashimono*, must have been used. Indeed, disasters and wars are two sides of the same coin in terms of stage direction and technology.

---

6   Kabuki shimpô, no. 1605, September 1894.

7   Miyako Shimbun, June 6, 1904.

Finally, I would like to consider the factors surrounding the popularity of such productions during the late Tokugawa period and the Meiji era. There is no doubt that a desire for realistic expression through Kabuki existed during this period, or in the art of the same period, including paintings. However, this may be thoroughly discussed in future studies. What I would like to simply point out, as a technical or theater history issue, is that the Kabuki stage expanded during this period. In the early 19th century, from 1804 to 1818, Nakamura-za, the most prestigious Kabuki playhouse in Edo, had a frontage of about 20 m—not the size of a theater but that of a stage. The oldest surviving Kabuki theater, Kanamaru-za, is said to have been constructed in 1835 to imitate the size and structure of the Ônishi theater in Dôtonbori, Osaka. The width of the hut itself is about 23.6 m, and that of the stage is about 10.9 m. On the other hand, the stage in Shintomi-za, which was opened in 1878, is about 14.5 m. In Kabuki-za, which opened in 1889, the stage expands to about 27.3 m. Large-scale theaters required spectacles that attracted the attention of many spectators, and the expansion of stage space allowed for such large-scale productions.

The end of the Tokugawa period and the Meiji era was a major turning point in the history of Kabuki theater as well as that of direction.

References

Hioki, Takayuki (2016): Hembô suru jidai no naka no kabuki: Bakumatu meijiki kabukishi, Tokyo: Kasama shoin.

Kawatake, Shigetoshi, ed. (1929): Nihon gikyoku zenshû, vol. 32, Tokyo: Shun'yôdô.

Kawatake, Shinshichi II et al. (n. d.): Ichibannori meiki-no sashimono (Engeki daichô 222-225). Manuscript owned by National Diet Library, Tokyo.

Kimura, Kinka (1943): Morita Kan'ya, Tokyo: Shin taishûsha.

Kokuritsu gekijô chôsa yôseibu, ed. (2013 [1860]): Kohada-no kaii ame-no furunuma, Tokyo: Japan Arts Council.

Kokuritsu gekijô chôsa yôseibu, ed. (2015 [1851]): Higashiyama sakura zôshi, Tokyo: Japan Arts Council.

Tamura, Nariyoshi, ed. (1976 [1922]): Zoku-zoku kabuki nendaiki: Ken-kan, Tokyo: Ôtori shuppan.

Berlin and its Theatres between 1870 and 1890[1]

ITODA Soichiro

We start with a look at a chart (fig. 1) showing the change in the number of theaters in Berlin from the 1850s to the 1930s. Two periods of significant increase can be seen from the end of the 1860s up to the early 1870s and from the end of the 1890s up to 1910. As the first of these periods represents the greatest expansion, this one will, however, take "center stage".

Although far more theaters did spring up during the first period of growth, only theaters that remained for more than one year following approval by the authorities are included here. This chart (fig. 2) shows the actual number of theaters approved, based on data from the Berlin Commercial Inspectorate (Gewerbepolizei). For the years 1869 and 1870, as many as 71 theater approvals are on record. According to Kunitake Kume's *True Account of the Ambassador Extraordinary & Plenipotentiary's Journey of Observation Through the United States of America and Europe*, the members of the so-called "Iwakura Mission" visited Berlin in 1873 and were quite surprised to find its citizens eating and drinking even during performances. This was something they never observed either in the theaters of New York, London, Paris, London or in any other theaters they visited during their month-long journey with the aim of studying political, social, economic and technological structures, hoping to gain insights that would be helpful in modernizing Japan and bringing it on par with western countries.

This sudden increase of theaters was caused by the "right of unrestricted commerce" (Gewerbefreiheit) introduced in 1869. The revised "Article 32" of the "Act on Theater Approval" states that "To open a theatrical business requires approval. Unless there are serious considerations concerning the liability of

---

1   The text is based on the third chapter of my book "Berlin & Tokyo – Theater und Hauptstadt" (Itoda 2008: 89-129). I would like to thank the publisher iudicium for their permission to use excerpts of it.

the applicant any application must be granted. Restricting theater performances to a certain genre is not permitted."[2] Prior to the introduction of the new right to unrestricted commerce it was up to the authorities to decide if there was demand for new commercial enterprises or not which allowed them to both limit the number of theaters and to specify theater locations at will. Now theaters could be opened with no regard to demand. The restriction on performing "tragedy, opera and ballet," a privilege that only the court theater had been granted up to then, was abandoned in the same act, together with restrictions concerning the nearest distance a new theater was allowed to be built around the court theater, in order not to become a competitor to its business. The same document shows that as many as 22 applications for opening a new theater had been denied between 1866 and 1868, amounting to 10 in 1867 alone. One can see that applications had considerably increased even before the revision of "Article 32" of the "Act on Theater Approval."

In True Account of the Ambassador Extraordinary & Plenipotentiary's Journey of Observation Through the United States of America and Europe, we are told that the "theaterscape" of Berlin had an atmosphere to be found in no other city in Europe or the United States. But what was it that made it so unique? Let's take a closer look at an article published on October 17th 1869, in "Kladderadatsch," a then popular German satirical magazine. This article was addressed to the editor-in-chief of the magazine and was posted by a fictional pub owner called "Bonekamp":

> Our customers are decreasing day by day. The number of theaters in Berlin this Sunday has already reached 23, and if you look at any of the flyers of 17 of those theaters, you can see that only one side of these "theater programs" lists plays or shows, whereas the other is nothing but a menu for food and drinks. If this doesn't stop, our business will perish. These "theaters" are nothing but low-class drinking establishments having a stage attached in order to get approval as theaters. One customer came to my pub last night, ordered a small bottle of beer and said, "What's on tonight?" As I thought he asked about food I said, "How about sauerbraten and dumplings?" But the customer said, 'No, I want to know what's on tonight!" to which I replied "Schafskopf, Klabberjass and 66. A hand of Whist might be played as well." The customer however said "No, stupid, not cards, I want to know what show

---

2   Bundesgesetzblatt des Norddeutschen Bundes (Journal of Law of the North German Confederation), No. 26, Berlin 1869.

is on today!" When I told him, "At my pub such performances are not done yet," he just said "I see," took his hat and left. I was really upset, could not sleep all night, and finally gave up my resistance. I would follow suit and set up a stage in my own pub as well.³

The article further reveals that the publican got the idea to use his apprentices as actors, to allow customers to mingle with actors on stage, and to even start writing some plays himself. The magazine "Kladderadatsch" thus satirizes the liberalization of the right to open theaters which had fired up competition so enormously and had even allowed cheap places to be approved as theaters. Prior to the amendment to the right to unrestricted commerce, there was a clear line that distinguished theaters from taverns, bars, or *Café-chantants* (singing cafés). At *Café-chantants* up to two persons were allowed to sing or tell sketches, but to perform full length plays as well as appearing in costumes on stage was not allowed at all. With the liberalization to open theaters due to the revision of the Commercial Law, all of these restraints were lifted.

This development also changed the traditional concept of what "theater was supposed to be" into something ambiguous and less distinct, and this ambiguity gave theaters a bad name. In 1873, a police notice requested "a crackdown" against such cheap theatrical venues in order to "protect public order and morals." The police also requested that the title "officially recognized theater" (konzessioniertes Theater) should only be granted to "real theaters" (wirkliche Theater), a term used to refer to theaters with regular admission fees and regularly scheduled programs. It can be said that the term "real theater" was created out of concerns for public safety. Only theaters that passed facility checks as well as fire prevention equipment checks would be allowed to call themselves "real theaters." Provisions referring to the safety of theaters in Berlin were listed in 1851 in a Police Ordinance wherein "Article 7" stipulates that authorities can make requests concerning 'safety, morals, security and business matters' when certifying theaters. Strict inspections were to be carried out to reduce the risk of fire on theater premises, and costs were to be shouldered by the theater's owner. According to the police ordinance of 1873, inspections were used as a tool to closely monitor theater buildings and safety measures. The effectiveness of this ordinance is reflected in the fact that, with

---

3   Bohnekamp 1869. About the right to establish a theatrical venue, and about economic freedom. Letter to the editors of the magazine "Kladderadatsch" written by Bohnekamp, owner of a wheat beer pub (in Berlin).

the exception of the new "Ostend-Theater" in 1877, no application was granted in the 1870s.

Let me give you some more details about Berlin's theater locations. This chart (fig. 3) shows theater locations from 1869 to the end of the 1870s. The black circles marked 1 and 2 are the court opera and the court theater. All black circles designate already existing theaters, and the white squares depict new theaters being built during this period. "Ostend-Theater," the aforementioned theater, is no. 16. As Berlin's city walls were demolished in the 1850s they do not appear on the map, but black circle no. 3 designates "Friedrich-Wilhelm-Theater," which was the first theater approved as a privately-owned theater within the then existing city walls. This location here in Schumann-Straße (Schumann Street) shows where "Deutsches Theater" ("German Theater") was built in the 1880s, a theater that would soon after completion play an important role in shaping the theater culture of Berlin. As I mentioned earlier, the introduction of the 'right of unrestricted commerce' in 1869 resulted in theaters shooting up all over Berlin, but the venues indicated by the white squares are only those that managed to survive for more than one year. Some of these theaters were not only maintained for more than one year but were still existent at the beginning of the 20th century, and some of them operated even until the 1920s and 30s. Of course, during that time both the name and appearance of many of these theaters changed, as did the owners and renters, but the location of these theaters plays a significant role in shaping Berlin's theatrical history. Dresdener-Straße (Dresden Street, no. 18 and 19) in Luisenviertel (Luisen Quarter) and Belle-Alliance-Straße (Belle-Alliance Street, no. 21) outside the Hallesches Tor (Hallesches Gate) form the center of theater developments in southern Berlin. The theaters of the northern Kastanienallee (Chestnut Boulevard, no. 15) and of Schönhauser Straße (Schönhaus Street, no. 25) survived until being turned into cinemas in the late 1910s, making this area a popular northern theater location for many years. Alongside the already existing "Werner-Theater" the new "Norbach-Theater," the predecessor of the 'Residenz-Theater' in eastern Blumenstraße (Flower Street), was the most prominent venue of Berlin's eastern theater development. After actor and theater director Bernhard Rose moved to "Ostend-Theater" (16) in Große Frankfurter Straße (Great Frankfurt Street) in the early 20th century, other theaters followed suite and the street became the most coveted location for "Volkstheater" (popular theater) buildings. With the implementation of the "right to unrestricted commerce" the definition of what "theater was supposed to mean," what theatrical venues should look like, and where they should be located had changed dramatically. In the 1880s, reactions against this development resulted in the enactment of new and much stricter theater policies.

As you can see in fig. 1 the number of theaters, which had increased enormously after the introduction of the "right of unrestricted commerce" in 1869, started to decrease in the 1880s. Here you see a map of theater locations from the 1880s, with the black triangle symbol indicating facilities that disappeared or lost the title "theater" during this period. With the exception of number 11, which indicates the "Alhambra-Theater," all of them were closed between the years of 1881 and 1883.

One of the most important changes concerns fire prevention. A new fire prevention ordinance was implemented in June of 1881. It is called 'General Instructions of District Police on Fire Prevention in Theaters of Berlin (Allgemeine ortspolizeiliche Vorschriften ueber die Feuerpolizei in den Theatern Berlins). In December of that year, the catastrophic fire at the "Wiener-Ring-Theater" (Vienna Ring Theater) shook Europe, as a result of which the Ministry of the Interior of "Norddeutscher Bund" ("North German confederation") issued a special ordinance to commissioners of Police of all cities inside its borders. The ordinance declared that "It is necessary to protect the audience" and to "Immediately take any measures that may be considered." As specific measures it listed "thorough investigation" of "fire extinguishing equipment, corridors, stairs, and exit structures, facilities for reliably shutting off fire, gas equipment inside buildings, and lighting for corridors."[4] After an inspection in June of 1881, structural weak points that were considered to endanger spectators in "Tonhalle Theater" (Hall of Sounds, no. 22) were described as follows: "In the event of a fire inside the theater, spectators on each floor (of the three-storied structure) must pass through the staircase and courtyard in front of the hall, and further through the front door. / What is more problematic about this theater is that if a fire breaks out in the front door and people panic, there will be no exit for the audience at all."[5] In light of the above-mentioned issues regarding the evacuation of spectators in the event of a fire, improvements were ordered as follows: "The ground floor must be eight meters wide and will be constructed as a passage way without doors. / In order to evacuate spectators from the 2nd and 3rd floors, there must be strongly built special

---

[4] Landesarchiv Berlin [Regional archive Berlin], Rep. 30 Berlin C Polizeipräsidium [Police head quarter] Title 74, Th 241: Feuersicherheiten in den Theatern [Fire prevention measures for theaters] 1846-82, p. 72.

[5] Regional archive Berlin, Th 498: Tonhalle, p. 16.

staircases on the left and right sides of the hall and on the side wings of the upper floors, which lead directly to the courtyard. / Buildings in front of the plot must be separated from the theater itself by solid walls without doors."[6] This document also specifies a deadline, stating that "the above measures must be implemented at the latest by October 15th 1873. In the event that the deadline is not met the theater will be shut down." On December 18th, theater owner Ferdinand Rosseck submitted two plan drawings to provide "emergency exits" in order to get police approval. The Police Fire Department did not reject Rosseck's drawings but ordered him to make additional improvements: "1. The exit of the stairs must lead directly to the courtyard. 2. The exit from the second or third floor must be twice as wide as the stairs. Doors must be set up by punching out walls to open into the garden. 4. The roof above the stage space must be provided with two ventilation valves with openings of about 4 square meters, the ventilation valves must be set up so that they can be opened by children at any time."[7] The demanding to build so many additional structures to ensure the safety of spectators was deemed necessary after the aforementioned fire catastrophe at the "Wiener-Ring-Theater." As Ferdinand Rosseck's "Tonhalle" did not meet the deadline set for October 15th, he was informed that starting December 14th, the place was no longer allowed to operate as a theater. "Tonhalle" had been known as the "Tonhalle-Theater" since it was granted approval in 1869 but became known as "Etablissement-Tonhalle" (Variety Theater) after being banned from putting on theater performances. The black triangles represent the theaters that lost their licence between 1880 and 1889 (fig. 4). In line with this transition, Ferdinand Rosseck, who had held the title of "Schauspielunternehmer" (theater entrepreneur), was afterwards just referred to as "Schankwirt" (publican). "Tonhalle" was a dance and song hall with no fixed seats and as such one of the theatrical venues that lost their right to call themselves "theater".[8]

The decline of the number of theaters in the 1880s was due not only to tightened regulations regarding the buildings that housed the theaters, but also to tighter rules concerning the business side, which made it even more difficult to obtain a license for opening a new theater. Since the beginning of

---

6 Ibid., p. 28.
7 Ibid., p. 31.
8 See the photography of the interior of "Tonhalle Theater" (Hall of Sounds Theater) in Jansen 1990.

the 1880s, an intensifying debate over the revision of "Article 32" of the Business Law was going on throughout Germany. The details of this debate can be found in the records of the German Reichstag, but here I will only highlight the most important points. The revised "Article 32" of the Business Law stated that "to open a theatrical business requires approval. Unless there are serious considerations concerning the liability of the applicant any application must be granted." This provision had let to a dramatic increase in the number of theaters since 1869. In the 1880s, this part was revised again as follows: "Theatrical performers need authorization to conduct business. It is the responsibility of the authority in charge to make sure that the business to be approved of is in compliance with requirements of morals, arts and finances. If there are reasons for doubt concerning an applicant's liability it must be denied."[9] In 1869, the emphasis was on "must be granted," but the amended text changed that term to "must be denied" if deemed necessary, thus giving the authorities greater discretion in denying an approval. The following reasons for this amendment were given by a proponent in the Imperial Parliament session of March 17th 1880:

> Freedom of business has led to an increase in theaters but has also led to a decline of the quality of German theaters. Theater managers are often nothing but pub owners who sell drinks alongside some theater performances staged in their pubs. With flimsy farces and bands playing light-hearted pieces of music, such theaters aim at attracting the masses. Even if the contents of those texts are not particularly obscene, they often contain expressions of vulgar speech and low regards for morality. / I do not think that this application for an amendment will improve the situation and will eliminate such evils at all. However, we do propose this amendment, because we do not see the necessity to allow non-professionals to run a theater at all. We want to give the word "trustworthy" used in these provisions a positive meaning and give the authorities in charge greater discretion in denying an approval. This means however that they must explain the reasons for doing so.[10]

After implementation, the amendment did not initially seem successful in eliminating the danger of "giving permission to everybody wanting to become a theater manager" at all. This changed only in 1883 when businesses

---

9 Steno-Berichte des Deutschen Reichstags [Stenographic reports of the German Parliament], March 17,1880, p. 69.
10 Ibid., p. 69.

that would be called "theater" and businesses designated as "non-theater" businesses were treated separately. The government stipulated "Article 33a" as an amendment to "Article 33," which originally regulated the businesses of restaurants and similar facilities and tried to make the distinction more explicit. The first part of this article states: "All kinds of musical performances, shows, drama performances or any other kinds of entertainments that are of no great value concerning arts and enlightenment must be shown in restaurants or similar spaces. Anyone who wishes to do so, even if already in possession of a license qualifying them as a theater entrepreneur, will hitherto need a special license." (Jansen 1990: 68) Since "Article 33" regulates restaurants and similar facilities, authorities could adjust the number of permits in a given area based on demand. This article thus allowed to limit the number of "singing halls" referred to as "Tingeltangel," and to protect theaters licensed under "Article 32" from the possible competition of such facilities.

It was, however, not easy to distinguish non-theaters like "entertainment places" (Etablissements), from theaters with "high regard for moral and artistic values." For example, when Franz Dorn became its impresario in 1886 the "Wintergarten Theater" (Wintergarten-Varieté-Theater, no. 28) was given approval as a theater venue under the condition that "artistic values must always be considered when performing." But impresario Dorn, who wanted to stage a wide variety of performing arts at "Wintergarten Theater," found that such constraints posed quite a challenge: "We constantly try to do what the law asks us to do, but it is difficult." In order to comply with Article 32, he therefore asked that a special clause be added to Article 33a that would allow "songs and plays" in which "those artistic values are not always clearly noticeable", which was granted.[11] "Wintergarten Theater" opened as an annex to Central Hotel which was built in the 1880s in the close vicinity of Friedrichstraße-Station, an urban elevated railway. "Wintergarten Theater" was located in the hotel's "winter garden," from which it took its name. The building was rectangular, and the roof had an arched dome made of glass to capture natural light. In the center of the picture, you can see the cafeteria, from which it was possible to watch the performances on the left stage while eating and drinking. A balcony was set up in the back, which overlooked the entire garden-like space with its variety of plants alongside the hotel's corridor. The theater is also famous for the first public and commercial cinema show in Germany in 1895, which was part of its variety program.

---

11 Landesarchiv Berlin, Th 1440, Wintergarten, p. 8.

As theaters and non-theaters were treated as different types of businesses both entertainment aspects as well as literary and artistic aspects became important for commercial theaters. In cooperation with "distinguished performing artists" Adolph L'Arronge, who had acquired the land of the former "Friedrich-Wilhelm-Straße-Theater," opened in 1883 "Deutsches Theater" ("German Theater", no. 3). The theater has a horseshoe-shaped seating capacity for 1600 people, indicating a preference for a "closed and focused space" like that found in "Hoftheater" (Court Theater). The design of the garden is not given much thought, but the "fire-resistant" structure of the theater is particularly emphasized in the application for approval. "The new theater uses non-flammable materials and is using electric lighting instead of gas lighting to eliminate the risk of fire." (Dreifuss 1987:57) The exterior of the Lessing Theater, which was established in 1888, has a stately appearance resembling that of the Imperial National Theater, and the interior structure includes "wide corridors", "many doors", and "many exits" to the outside. (Freydank 1988: 307) It appears to have incorporated the modifications of the 1889 Fire Ordinance. The "Lessing Theater" is built in an open space alongside Friedrich-Karl-Ufer, a Spree riverside street, a location apparently chosen with consideration of the heightened security concerns of the 1880s. Lessing Theater was especially famous for staging works of "contemporary playwrights." In the 1880s the "German Theater" as well as the "Lessing Theater" and the "Berlin Theater" (no. 8), which is located on the land of the former "Walhalla Variety Theater", were founded. These three theaters are the most representative venues of Berlin's theatrical scene in the 1880s.

In the 1880s, the provisions of the law were powerful enough both to separate theater from non-theater businesses and to help create a new style of theaters and of theatrical repertoire. In 1888, Maximilian Harden's article "Berlin as Theater Capital, Berlin in 1888" ("Berlin als Theaterhauptstadt, Berlin 1888") was published. In this article, the author probes Berlin's potential as a "theater capital" in Europe, surpassing even Paris and London. He also points out the opening of the above-mentioned three theaters. For Harden the relationship between institutions and culture was a reciprocal one that makes it irrelevant to ask which one precedes which. It is, however, no exaggeration to say that, in the 1800s, changes concerning the structural and the business side of theaters, combined with changes concerning artistic requirements, contributed, to quite a large extent, in giving Berlin's theaters a new outlook.

References

Bohnekamp (1869): "Zur Theater- und Gewerbefreiheit: Schreibebrief des Weißbierlokalbesitzers Bohnekamp an die Redaktion des Kladderadatsch." In: Kladderadatsch Nr. 48, XXII Jahrgang, October 17, 1869.

Dreifuss, Alfred (1987): Deutsches Theater Berlin Schumannstraße 13a, Berlin: Henschel.

Freydank, Ruth (1988): Theater in Berlin: Von den Anfängen bis 1945 [Theater Berlin: From the beginnings until 1945], Berlin: Henschel.

Itoda, Soichiro (2008): Berlin & Tokyo: Theater und Hauptstadt [Berlin & Tokyo: Theater and Capital]. Munich: iudicium.

Jansen, Wolfgang (1990): Das Varieté, Berlin: Edition Hentrich.

Figures

If no other reference is listed the documents are taken from Itoda 2008.

Fig. 1: Number of Theaters from 1850 – 1930

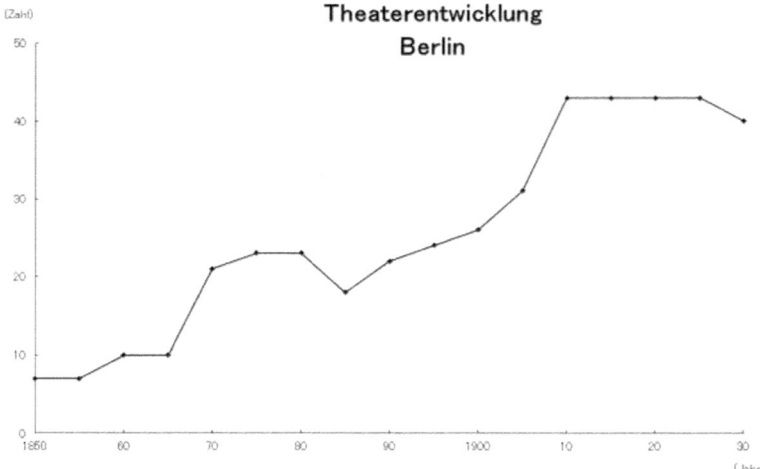

Fig. 2: Number of theater applications approved or denied before and after the implementation of the revised "Article 32" in 1869

資料2　営業法32条による劇場の認可数と不許可数

	認可数	不許可数
1848	5	3
1849	1	4
1850	1	3
1851	1	4
1852	2	3
1857	1	1
1858	1	2
1859	3	4
1860	1	4
1862	1	1
1865	2	2
1866	1	7
1867	?	10
1868	1	5
1869	34	9
1870	37	3
1871	14	1
1872	22	?

（出所）　ブランデンブルク州中央古文書館所蔵資料より。

Fig. 3 (above): Distribution of theaters from 1869 until the late 1870s;
Fig. 4 (below): Distribution of theaters between 1880 and 1889

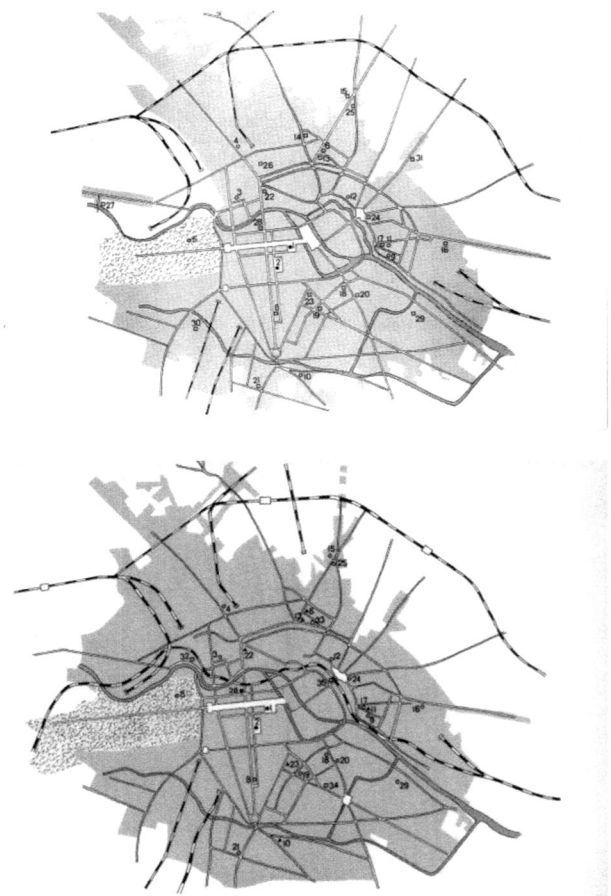

The Theatres in Modern Shanghai: From the Perspective of Cultural History[1]

ENOMOTO Yasuko

The heart of this thesis is a theatre with more than 150 years of history and tradition in Shanghai, China. The Lyceum Theatre (Chinese name: Lanxin Daxiyuan 蘭心大戯院) was known as the "Western Arts Hall of Fame" in Shanghai until the end of World War II. There is the special situation of Shanghai behind this, which has evolved as a western concession; at the same time, however, it has something in common with the modernization of theatres found throughout Asia. From 2010 to 2016, I participated in research specifically for the Lyceum Theatre in the KAKENHI Joint Research Group[2]. What I report here is part of that research.

1. China Modernization and Shanghai Settlement

Before introducing the Lyceum Theatre, let us review where Shanghai is. Shanghai is located where the Yangtze River (揚子江) pours into the sea and had favorable conditions for trade, making it a base for European and American powers and Japan to enter the continent. The British won the Opium War in 1842 and attained the Qing Dynasty, opening five ports, including Shanghai, and colonizing Hong Kong. China's modernity began with this external pressure, and the settlements set up in Shanghai developed

---

1 This article is related to my Japanese-language essay,: Enomoto 2018.
2 JSPS KAKENHI Grant Number JP23320050 „History and Symbols of the Shanghai Foreign Settlements Theater Culture: A Multilingual Cross-Sectional Study of the Lyceum Theatre" (2011-2014) and JSPS KAKENHI Grant Number JP26284036 „A Study on the Continuity of the Theatre Arts of Shanghai Settlements in the 1940s and the Aspects of Spread of the Arts into Other Regions" (2014-2017). In each case, the principal investigators are ÔHASHI Takehiko, a professor at Kwansei Gakuin University.

as a special area beyond China's sovereignty. By the end of the 19th century, Shanghai had the International Settlement, run mainly by the British; the city also had the French Concession, managed by the French government, where Chinese as well as foreigners could live. Until the end of World War II, Shanghai flourished as an international city with people of different ethnicities and nationalities.

Regarding politics, earlier Shanghai was a land dominated by imperial powers in the background of armed forces. However, regarding cultural history, it was a place where a unique modern culture combining the West and East had been born. Foreign culture first came to Shanghai, was given a Chinese character by the people of Shanghai, and then spread throughout China. It is no exaggeration to say that the history of modern Chinese music, dance, drama, and movies all began in Shanghai.

2. Lyceum Theatre History

Next, let us discuss the history of the Lyceum Theatre.

The Lyceum Theatre was built in 1866 as a dedicated theatre for the British Amateur Dramatic Club. While working in the opium and tea trades, British living in Shanghai rehearsed plays, practiced music in their spare time, and held recitals. During a time when foreign residents were few and entertainment was scarce, it was a valuable pleasure to play by themselves and watch one another's performances with friends. They built the theatre because they wanted a place for continuous recreational activities, and building a Western-style theatre signified confirmation of their Western identity. Lyceum Theatre bears the same name as the theatre in London; in Shanghai, there was a desire to match London's artistry.

A fire destroyed and forced the Lyceum Theatre, to relocate in 1874, and the second generation was built. In 1931, the third generation relocated to the Shanghai French Concession. You can still see it on Maoming South Road (茂名南路) in central Shanghai. The third generation has a medium capacity of 723 people and is a theatre designed for drama, but it was also used as a venue for performances of opera companies and artists from Europe with the development of concessions and entertainment commercialization. Since

1934, it has also been the venue for regular concerts of the Shanghai Municipal Orchestra.[3]

During the Russian Revolution, Shanghai had become home to a number of White Russian artists who fled the revolution. The Russian upper class could speak French, so the French Concession in Shanghai seemed a convenient place to live. The Russians also performed operas and ballets while reminiscing about their homeland, and the Lyceum Theatre became known as a stage for Russian art.

In the late 1930s, Jewish refugees who fled Nazi Germany also settled in Shanghai, and artists who were active in Vienna and elsewhere appeared at the Lyceum Theatre. Shanghai was a valuable place in the world, offering these refugees a space to continue their artistic activities.[4]

A distinctive feature of the Lyceum Theatre was that Westerners living in Shanghai operated it to maintain their culture. Most people on the stage were Westerners, as were majority of the audiences. However, since the 1930s, the social status of Chinese people has improved, and intellectuals and wealthy people who had returned home after studying in Europe and the United States gradually started coming to the theatre. In other words, as the times passed, the Lyceum Theatre began to play an enlightening role in expressing to the Chinese what Western art was. It seems difficult to understand drama because of language restrictions, but music and dance had the advantage of being easily transmitted to people of any country.

The Lyceum Theatre was also a special place for the Japanese. In Japan, the Shanghai boom began in the 1920s, propelling Shanghai as a popular place to experience Western culture and customs without going to Europe. Famous writers, such as AKUTAGAWA Ryûnosuke, visited Shanghai one after another and published travelogues. Western arts such as orchestras and ballets were regularly performed, and their blending into citizens' daily lives more than that in Tokyo provided Japanese artists with much to study.

When the Pacific War began in 1941, Japanese troops were stationed in the Shanghai International Settlement, expelling the British and Americans. As the Japanese took over the management of the Lyceum Theatre, Japanese artists experienced increased stage time. ASAHINA Takashi, who later became a global conductor, also experienced a high level of performance by Rus-

---

3   For the history of the Shanghai Municipal Orchestra, see Enomoto 2006.
4   For more information on the characteristics and realities of the Shanghai music world, see Iguchi 2019.

sian artists for the first time, as a guest at a regular concert of the Shanghai Philharmonic Orchestra (former Shanghai Municipal Orchestra). In addition, Komaki Masahide—the only Japanese member of the Russian ballet company, Ballet Russe, at the time—took many performances from Shanghai back to Japan after the war, contributing to the development of ballet in Japan [5].

3   The Role of Western Theatre in Asia

Shanghai is different from other cities in China in that it has developed rapidly with foreign investment since the mid-19th century. Foreigners also made buildings that serve as urban infrastructure and landmarks during the settlement era. At the time, the British believed Shanghai lacked cultural facilities and buildings. In the 20th century, however, the land prices in central Shanghai were quite high and the population was overcrowded, preventing the construction of new, large buildings such as opera houses. Incidentally, France built several opera houses in Indochina, which was their colony, but the Shanghai French Concession had no official cultural facilities other than a few schools and clubs.

In the 1930s, Shanghai was the sixth largest city in the world with a population of over 3 million, but there was no other theatre specializing in Western performing arts as the Lyceum Theatre was. There were only large and small theatres that presented traditional plays. In the late 1940s, there were 128 theatres in Shanghai, 40 of which were also used as cinemas, and 81 were dedicated to Chinese traditional drama (Wang 2008). A well-known example is Theatre Grand (Chinese name: Daguangming Daxiyuan大光明大戲院). This was the finest cinema presenting Hollywood movies and was sometimes used for orchestra performances. However, regarding sound effects, it seems that it was not suitable for non-movie use.

The growth of new entertainment such as movies, music, and drama performances at the Lyceum Theatre struggled to attract audiences. However, the reason the theatre had maintained despite lower profits was its symbolic implications for foreign residents as a hall of Western art.

In fact, theatres with similar functions were built in other colonies and settlements in Asia. In 1870, for example, a British-led amateur dramatic

---

5   See Enomoto (2015) on the relationship between the Japanese and the Lyceum Theatre.

group created the Gaiety Theatre, which existed in the Yokohama settlement in Japan. Initially, most of the British who came to Yokohama immediately after the opening of the port were traditionally trading in Shanghai, so they worked in the same way as they did in Shanghai—created communities and performed leisure activities such as drama. The Gaiety Theatre was relocated in 1885, and the second generation was constructed. Shakespeare dramas and other works presented there influenced Japanese writers and artists. However, it was destroyed by a fire during the Great Kanto Earthquake of 1923 and was never rebuilt.

Regarding the UK base in Asia, Hong Kong cannot be forgotten. Hong Kong developed as a British colony after the Opium War and had more residents than Shanghai at the end of the 19th century. Jardine Matheson & Co., which had made significant profits in the opium trade, donated to build City Hall, inside of which was a large theatre called Theatre Royal. There is also a music hall called St. Andrews Hall (Nakamura 1993: 646). These were opened in 1869, approximately at the same time as the first Lyceum Theatre in Shanghai and the Gaiety Theatre in Yokohama. The Suez Canal was opened in 1869, and the route has been significantly shortened since then, with more artists visiting Asia from Europe. Not only performers, but also opera companies, circus companies, etc., have been traveling around Asia for a long time.

In the past, research on how Western music was accepted in Asia has traditionally been regarded as a modernization problem of Japan and China. The late Nakamura, Rihei was the first to break down the narrow framework, and he vigorously investigated materials such as English newspapers and official documents in various parts of Asia, highlighting that there was a music market connected to East Asia by sea route at the end of the 19th century.

I followed Nakamura's approach to English newspaper, *The North China Herald*—published in Shanghai—and examined music concert ads and reviews. The results showed that the number of concerts in Shanghai began to increase significantly in 1874, in line with the opening of the second-generation Lyceum Theatre. In other words, if there is a good theatre with the potential for box office revenue, more Westerners will consider incorporating Shanghai into a performance tour. The existence of the theatre attracted European artists to Asia.

According to Nakamura's research, in addition to Shanghai and Hong Kong, there was also the Town Hall in Singapore, Gymnasium Theatre in Kobe, and Public Hall in Nagasaki (ibid.). All of these facilities were originally created for residents' recreational activities but were also gradually rented out for the outside artists' performances.

Let us compare Nakamura's research with previous research on Yokohama Gaiety Theatre and examine specific examples. The first Gaiety Theatre in Yokohama was overly small and the facilities were not high quality. However, thanks to the construction of the second generation in 1885, two opera companies came to Japan that year. The first was the Mascot Opera Company, which toured Singapore → Hong Kong → Shanghai → Kobe → Yokohama → Hong Kong → Shanghai with multiple performances in Yokohama from August 25 to September 19. The works of popular operetta composers in Europe, including Gilbert and Sullivan's *The Pirates of Penzance: The Slave of Duty* and *Patience: / Bunthorne's Bride* as well as Lecock's *La Fille de Madame Angot*, were performed (Nakamura 1993: 652; Masumoto 1986: 218-219).

The second, Emelie Melville Opera Company, toured Hong Kong → Shanghai → Kobe → Yokohama → Kobe, with several performances in Yokohama from November 10 to 27. Bizet's *Carmen* was brought to the head of the series (ibid.). It was also a characteristic of the time that performances were performed again as the company traveled back home. As each region's reputation rose, the return journey would have become increasingly popular as "Triumphal Performances."

Guillaume Sauvlet, a Dutch pianist living in Shanghai who visited Japan with Mascot Opera Company, served not only as a piano accompanist for the opera company but also held several solo concerts at the Yokohama Gaiety Theatre. Eventually, he separated from the opera company and settled in Japan. In 1886, he was expected his ability and became a foreign teacher at Ongaku Torishirabe-gakari, Japan's first music education institution.

Foreign teachers have played a major role in modernizing music education in both Japan and China. However, researchers had little interest in where and how the foreign teachers originated, and it was unknown that foreigners came and went between Shanghai and Yokohama. From a Western perspective, both Shanghai and Yokohama were two of the many cities in East Asia, perhaps only chosen by settlers for their valuable jobs. In the future, research will be needed not only from the perspective of accepting Western music in Asia, but also from the perspective of global movement and flow of Western music.

4. Localization of Western Theatre Culture

Lastly, let us discuss the specialty of Shanghai and the theatre culture that was born there.

Shanghai was an Asian terminal where multiple sea routes intersected, and there was the International Settlement—an area that remained politically neutral without belonging to any state. Thanks to this, people, goods, and money came and went freely from a wide area of Europe, the United States, and Asia, and the city was full of various cultures. It can be said that the Chinese in Shanghai took full advantage of these geographical conditions and chose what they needed to form their own culture.

In the history of Chinese music and performing arts, folk songs and play music rooted in local cultures were at the center, and traditional local drama difangxi (地方戲), such as Peking Opera, was the most familiar entertainment for ordinary people. The traditional theatre was called chayuan (茶園), and tables were arranged between seats to watch the play while drinking tea. However, in 1908, "Xinwutai (新舞台)"—constructed in Shiliupu (十六舖), Shanghai—was the first modern theatre to remove all tables. According to Chen Linghong (陳凌虹)'s research (Chen 2014, Chapter 4, Section 2), Xinwutai was not a square stage supported by conventional pillars, but rather had a half-moon-shaped front with the pillars removed. In addition, it is said that it was possible to have snowflakes (confetti) fall from the rafters and running water on the stage, as well as a rotating stage, background writing, and props. The three-story building had a large capacity of 2,000 people, abolishing the conventional system where tea and theatre fees were not distinguished and succeeded in introducing a ticketing system.

Many Chinese students had studied modernization measures in Japan since the beginning of the 20th century, and the construction of the new stage was influenced by Japanese theatres. In Japan, Western theatres—which were similar to the European opera houses—were expected by the European policy at the end of the 19th century. Shintomiza, with gas lamps and chair seats, and Yurakuza, the base for new plays, have been constructed in succession. Chinese students experienced Western-style theatres and modern drama in Tokyo and started working on modern drama performances of their own. The first theatre group Chunliushe (春柳社) in modern China was formed in Tokyo.

The intellectuals who returned from studying abroad, and those who were influenced by them, also participated in modern drama in Shanghai. In 1908, a group called Chunyangshe (春陽社) held a performance at the second-generation Lyceum Theatre. According to Xu Banmei (徐半梅), who played an active part in the theatrical scene at the time, the sound effects of the Lyceum Theatre were excellent, and whispering dialogue on the stage reached the third floor.[6] Many actors would love the excellent facilities at the Lyceum Theatre, but the Chinese troupe could not perform regularly, likely because of the high rents.

The Chinese entered the Lyceum Theatre numerous times after the Japanese army ruled Shanghai in the 1940s during the Pacific War. Because of the expulsion of the British and Americans, fewer people used the theatre, and the Japanese side of the theatre managed to lend to a Chinese troupe to make money. Since 1942, the Lyceum Theatre had been active in contemporary plays and original plays based on history, some of which had been a huge hit because of the hidden anti-Japanese message.[7] In sum, the drama performed by Westerners at the Lyceum Theatre did not affect the Chinese concerning content, but the existence of the Lyceum Theatre itself helped the development of modern Chinese drama.

It is rare for a study in Shanghai to focus on a single theatre, and our research group included not only English and Chinese newspapers, but also French and Russian newspapers. As the foreign language newspapers in the settlement era have been digitized in places such as the Shanghai Library, it is easy to collect information on specific theatres and performances in various languages for future research. If it is connected to not only Shanghai but also cities such as Hong Kong, Yokohama, and Singapore, it will become clear that the works and performances were transmitted as artists moved. Research on the acceptance, diffusion, and localization of Western art in Asia will must be understood as dynamism of the entire region, regardless of borders.

---

6   Xu 1957, p. 4.

7   Seto 2015. The performance at that time was detailed by Shao 2012. In addition, see Zhao Yi "LanxinDaxiyuan shangyan yanmu yilanbiao(1941-1945)", Ohashi, Zhao, Enomoto and Iguchi ed. 2015, pp..243-294.

References

Chen, Linghong (2014): Nitchû engeki kôryû no shosô: Chûgoku kindai engeki no seiritsu, Kyoto: Shibunkaku shuppan.

Enomoto, Yasuko (2006): Shanhai ôkesutora monogatari: Seiyôjin ongakukatachi no yume, Tokyo: Shunjûsha.

Enomoto, Yasuko (2015): "Nihonjin ga Shanhai no gekijô de mita yume." In: Ajia yûgaku 183, pp. 51-62.

Enomoto, Yasuko (2018): "Gekijô kara miru Higashi Ajia no kindai bunka." In: Journal of the Faculty of Letters (Chuo University) 269, pp. 185-203.

Iguchi, Junko (2019): Bômeishatachi no Shanhai gakudan: Sokai no ongaku to baree, Tokyo: Ongaku no tomosha.

Masumoto, Masahiko (1986): Yokohama Gêteza: Meiji Taishô no seiyôgekijô (2nd ed.), Yokohama: Iwasaki hakubutsukan shuppankyoku.

Nakamura, Rihei (1993): Yôgaku dônyûsha no kiseki: Nihon kindai ongakushi josetsu, Tokyo: Tôsui shobô.

Ôhashi, Takehiko et al. (eds.) (2015) : Shanghai zujie yu Lanxin Daxiyuan, Shanghai: Shanghai renmin chubanshe.

Seto, Hiroshi (2015): "Raishamu gekijô (Ranshin daigiin) to Chûgoku wageki: Shanhai rengeigekisha 'Buntenshô' o chûshin ni." In: Ajia yûgaku 183, pp. 112-122.

Shao, Yingjian (2012): Shanghai kangzhan shiqi de huaju. Beijing: Peking University Press.

Wang, Huiqing: "Shanghai xiyuan de yanbian." In: Shanghai dang'an guan xinxi wang, April 1, 2008 (retrieved January 10, 2020, http://www.archives.sh.cn/shjy/scbq/201203/t20120313_6039.html).

Xu, Banmei (1957): Huaju chuangshiqi huiyilu. Beijing: Zhongguo xiju chubanshe.

Discussions on Theatre Spaces and Theatre Materials by the Leningrad School[1]

ITO Masaru

It is well known that the reformation of theatre practices accompanied the emergence of stage directors in the early 20th century. Meanwhile, in Russia, the focus shifted from drama text to stage in the late 19th century. By the early 20th century, friction between drama text and direction became conspicuous. The perspective change in theatre in practice—mainly in Europe—simultaneously caused a change in the study of the discipline. As scholar Erika Fischer-Lichte notes, these theoretical shifts encouraged Max Herrmann and others to produce 'theatre studies (*Theaterwissenschaft*)'. Herrmann-style theatre studies were imported into Russia while Russian-style theatre studies were formulated by the Leningrad School, through the Department of Theatre History at the Institute of Art History in Leningrad. In the 1920s, A. Gvozdev (1887–1939), the head of the Department of Theatre History in the Institute of Art History, played a central role in the development of the movement. In his 1924 thesis, *Results and Tasks of Theatre History Studies*, Gvozdev states the following:

> There is no doubt that the environment of general theatrical life in our time contributes to the establishment of a 'purely theatrical' point of view of research. The search for new ways of theatre at the end of the 19th century and at the beginning of the 20th century, which put forward the slogan 'theatricalisation of theatre' (Georg Fuchs) and revealed the practical possibilities of 'pure theatre', not only illuminated the historical past of theatre with a new bright light, but also created in society the mood on which the future theatre historian would be able to rely. (Gvozdev 1924: 85)

The activities of the Institute of Art History, as its name implies, were essentially historical studies. While Gvozdev and his colleagues positioned contem-

---

1   This article is based on a part of a paper published in Japanese: Ito 2020.

porary theatre in a historical context, they also anticipated its implications for the future. The scholar pointed out that these *new theatre ideas* were inspired not only by practicality but also by the involvement of researchers. Indeed, he notes:

> However, we should not overestimate the impact of the contemporary issues of theatrical life on scientific activities. [...] The renewal of theatre history studies comes not from practical innovative practitioners of theatre, but from the academic environment of laboratories in universities, which is not damaged by quarrels and debates about new theatre. (ibid: 85)

Despite an appreciation for contemporary theatre practice, Gvozdev proposed that an academic approach was needed, stating:

> There is no deeper disconnection between life practise and academic and aesthetic arguments than in theatre. Theatre people have repeatedly appealed for help to study on theatre, and have always been exposed to the formidable ignorance—nescimus—in front of them. [...] To change this situation is an urgent issue today. (ibid: 121)

Here, Gvozdev's use of the term 'nescimus' refers to the lack of knowledge about theatrical performance history, a subject neglected by theatre research as literary studies. Gvozdev opined that no existing language of literary studies can describe theatre performance as a union of various arts, and that if theatre practitioners pursue *autonomous theatre* (which is independent from text), a new language is required to interrogate it. He was trying to solve this problem using theatre history as a framework—or perhaps trying to decode theatre history from the aforementioned perspective.

Gvozdev describes the idea of 'original methods' as 'a major task of theatre history as an academic'. (ibid: 85) Researchers should remain cognisant that various elements that comprise theatre performance (such as stage design, costumes, acting, music, and audiences) have not been recognised as subjects by literary studies. When it comes to conducting such research, Gvozdev cites Max Herrmann as a pioneer. In his dissertation, Gvozdev discusses in detail Herrmann's *Research on the History of German Theatre of the Middle Ages and the Renaissance*, published in 1914.

According to Gvozdev, Herrmann's book is divided into two parts. The first is an effort to restore the *tragedy of Horn-skinned Siegfried* by Hans Sachs in 1557, which was performed at St. Malta's Church in Nuremberg. The second is dedicated to deciphering illustrations of the stage in the plays of Publius

Terentius and the books of Swiss Renaissance playwrights. (ibid: 92-93) In the first part, Herrmann derives the hypothesis of the size and form of the theatrical space from limited materials. He also tries to restore the virtual theatrical space and correct it by applying stage direction in the text related to that space. This method, which Gvozdev termed 'topographic projection' (топографическая проекция)(ibid: 94), enabled theatre history researchers to visualize an accurate spatial grasp, which Gvozdev then evaluated.

Herrmann reconstructed the space of the church where the play was performed, the location of the audiences, and the position of the performers. This was achieved by reading individual details from leftover materials and restoring the image in its entirety through this reading. Gvozdev noted that the Herrmann approach served 'to decisively distinguish theatre history from drama history' (ibid: 94). While Gvozdev praised Herrmann, he wrote that 'theatre—the stage, acting, directing, and the audience—is a factor of autonomous art that exists according to its own rule'. (ibid: 94) Herrmann's words, 'theatre art is an art of space' (*Theaterkunst ist eine Raumkunst*) became the rout from drama studies as a literary study to theatre studies as a study of performance. According to Gvozdev, 'researchers have a duty to consider the space in which stage actions are developed. Moreover, reconstruction of theatrical space is the first step toward defining the actors' movements, props, and the stage set'. (ibid: 94) As such, he attempted to describe theatre's *autonomy* [from text] from the perspective of academics. It refers to an attitude for analysing the kind of situation created by 'theatrical space' and how it forms 'performance'.

Gvozdev and other members of the Leningrad School regularly held seminars and conferences on theatre history at the Institute of Art History. They discussed various aspects of performance and published their conclusions in *On the Theatre*, which contained their annals of essays on the institute's Theatre History and Theatre Theories Division. For example, V. Solov'ev's 'The Performing of Things (вещи) in Theatre Performance' was a summary of a report at a public meeting held at the institute's Theatre History and Theatre Theories Division on 20 December 1925. The beginning of the thesis states the following: 'The illustrative part of the report was developed jointly with the chief of the Theatre Laboratory of the Institute, N. P. Izvekov'. (Solov'ev 1926: 51)[2]

Solov'ev also clarifies his position: 'If not so long ago the history of theatre was considered as the history of dramatic literature, nowadays the history of theatre is usually understood as the history of theatrical performances'. He also suggests that 'studying various elements individually leads the studies towards a one-sided consideration' and that there is a need for an 'axis' that enables the consideration as something that can integrate various elements discussed individually, something with mutual interaction. One element that may function as the 'axis' is 'things'. According to him, 'things in theatre performance' inhabited the stage long before actors recognised the role of costumes; furthermore, things are part of the stage's spatial design—they are also among the 'main elements of theatrical phenomena (*mise en scène* in French, *Incenierung* in German)'. (ibid: 51)

In this thesis, Solov'ev analyses the role of things in theatre performance, separating them into two categories: dynamic and static. The term 'dynamic' refers, in his words, to 'what directly joins in the play and exists on an equal footing with actors, as if it plays a special role without lines'. (ibid: 52) For example, it is 'Khlestakov's letter read in the last scene of Gogol's *The Government Inspector*, or the window where Podkolyosin jumps out in Gogol's *Marriage*'. (ibid: 52) In other words, if Khlestakov's letter and the window in *Marriage* disappear from the play, the performance would be interrupted and rendered incomplete. In some cases, it is not only the story's progress, but also the existence of the thing that defines the actor's existence and physicality on stage. For example, an object that is too large to exist in everyday life stipulates the physicality of the actor who performs with it and conveys a comical impression. Thus, theatre employs a number of things with 'purposes' in performance, and Solov'ev positions such things as 'dynamic'. (ibid: 52)

Regarding 'static' things, Solov'ev does not propose any specific functions and offers a general theory. To illustrate the concept of static things, he writes, 'there is a table in the parlour which shows that they are middle class. On one of the tables, we should find an album with photo cards, and on the walls there will be paintings, such as Kaulbach's *The Virgin Mary* or Böcklin's *Isle of the Dead*. (ibid: 52) Such things often appear during the performance even though 'no

---

2   At the actual time of the report, several assistants demonstrated the performance based on Solov'ev's report, and there is a brief supplementary commentary on the scene.

one even touches the album, and no one looks at the wall paintings'. (ibid: 52) In other words, these things do not play any role beyond portraying the characters as a middle-class family, and are not actively involved in the progress of the performance. Solov'ev places these things as 'static and have the meaning of decorative and descriptive'. (ibid: 52)

Solov'ev further states that, 'the whole history of the designing of things in theatrical space can probably be observed as a fierce struggle between these two principles'. (ibid: 52) Indeed, he contends that the dynamic existence of things that have a purpose on the stage precedes the static and decorative existence from a historical perspective. For example, regarding the comedy of Aristophanes, Solov'ev notes the various ways in which the purposeful state of things appear on stage.

In the Middle Ages, the use of decorative things became widespread in the practise of plays, which mainly consisted of enthusiasts and amateurs, and school theatre. During these shows, things abstracted various characters and were used to indicate the role played by characters on stage (for example, 'the one who administers the law has a balance and a blindfold over their eyes; the one who administers the truth has a mirror'. (ibid: 53)). In the tradition of ballet and opera, which emerged in the late 16th century, things on the stage were treated as though static use was the only option.

It was in Renaissance professional performances when things once again took on a dynamic and purposeful role. The theatre performances in this era, along with Italian impromptu comedies, were heavily influenced by mediaeval jongleur and histrion; they regained the dynamism that was forgotten in amateur performances. In Italian improvised comedy, props influenced the progress of scenes on the stage and set the direction for their evolution. As linguistic expression became dominant during the 18th and 19th centuries, progress on the stage leaned excessively toward the logical interpretation of play texts, and the presence of things in the performance was reduced to mere décor or 'accidental details' on the stage.

Solov'ev transcribes theatre history from the perspective of the existence of things on the stage, noting an extension of such theatre history in that modern times have once again shifted to the organic use of things. As an example, he refers to the implementation by Russian director Vs. Meyerhold (1874–1940) during that era. Solov'ev observes that the actors at the Meyerhold Theatre have high levels of physical ability and nourish their reflexes, thereby gaining an organic connection with things. For example, *the Forest* (A. Ostrovsky), which Meyerhold directed in 1924, shows a scene involving a maid, Aksyusha, and a territorial mistress, Gurmyzhskaya. Aksyusha is drying the laundry when 'the laundry pile, squeeze rolls, and wrinkle-stretching bars give the movements of the actress extreme conciseness and expressiveness. At the same time, these emphasise the importance of everything that is done on the stage'. (ibid: 58)

According to Solov'ev, the most important component in the use of things in these new theatrical tides can be seen in the villa in *A Profitable Position* (A. Ostrovsky), which was also directed by Meyerhold. In this work, staged in 1923, the villa where Zhadov and Pauline live was set up on constructivist scaffolds. There, the characters did not simply perform the appearance of the lives existing in the play. The construction of the villa, in Solov'ev's words, functioned as a 'complex theatre device' (сложный театральный прибор) (ibid: 59) and was a place to demonstrate the actors' physicality.

This attitude was shared by Gvozdev's 'On the Shift of Theatrical Systems' (Gvozdev 1926), which was included in the same collection of essays, *On the Theatre*. Here, Gvozdev transcribes theatre history in terms of stage structure. He discusses the characteristics of two basic types of stage space found between the 16th to 19th centuries: the 'court-style, box stage' and the 'temporary stage in the fair'. He discusses these two forms binarily, and from various perspectives, such as the relation between the actors' performance and the audience; moreover, he attempts to account for the history of a temporary stage that is not a box stage. Gvozdev, who constructs theatre history from the space of performance, states that space composition determines each condition on the stage.

For example, assume a 'night scene' is in progress; the lighting in a box stage can easily indicate that it is 'night'. One can use a technical device to create such an illusion (as the actor's personal abilities do not matter here). Conversely, on a fair stage, the success of the 'night scene' depends entirely on the professional skills and techniques of individual actors—even sunlight shining on them from above is assumed to be irrelevant. (ibid: 8-9) In addition, Gvozdev indicates that the dramaturgy changes accordingly. He says, 'on the fairground stages, it (dramaturgy) will rely on actors and offer him the necessary verbal material for the deployment of his performances, and more weight is placed on words that are understandable to audiences on the fairgrounds'. Alternatively, 'on a box stage, they aim to use all of the stage mechanisms, and match the taste of the selected audience who sit in armchairs and box seats in a richly decorated hall'. (ibid: 9)

Ultimately, Gvozdev considers that 'the system of theatre will be determined by the place of action, on the topographic conditions in which grows a theatrical performance designed for a certain stage area and a certain composition of audience that is closely related to this topography'. (ibid: 9) Based on this assertion, it may be said that the history of plays is not positioned in the literary history of the playwright's personal creation, but rather in terms of stage setting, and theatre history exists according to it.

Analysing such stage space as the axis for describing theatre history, Gvozdev further tries to describe the structure of the audience, the actor's performance, and the character of the dramaturgy that works for the actor in each 'correlation'. Notably, the primary concern here is the presence of a stage space, and the dramaturgy follows. This is reminiscent of the relationship between directors and drama text that has existed since the 20th century. Meyerhold often referred to himself as the 'author of performance', a stance in which the existing drama text was modified; consequently, he was criticised for blaspheming against the classics. Referring to Gvozdev's logic, Meyerhold's attempt has legitimacy 'in theatre history' precisely because the play exists due to the presence of stage space.

The problem, however, was that such history was forgotten during the early 20th century. 'There is currently no fair stage around us', Gvozdev said.

> Along with the growth of industrial capitalism in the 19th century, the fair as a factor of economic life is being destroyed. Along with the fair, the fairgrounds and the associated system of 'popular' theatre finally disappear. [...] However, the decisive disappearance of the system of 'popular' theatre must be compared with the crucial fact of our theatrical reality—the box stage is kept steady and included in the basics of the material in today's construction of theatre. [...] The establishment of the 'court' theatre system as a system of stage art in general in Europe, its triumph over the system of 'popular' theatre and the resulting 'separation from the people', so characteristic of theatre of the new era, thus have become the focus of attention of theatre sociologists and the central problem of scientific theatre studies. (ibid: 10-11)

From this problem of consciousness, predeclaring that it is just a 'rough outline', Gvozdev describes 'how the "box stage" of the court-style theatre was born, how it spread throughout Europe in a triumphal march, where and how it collided with the system of "popular" theatre, and how the struggle of the systems ended in each country' (ibid: 11) as the history of the struggle between the "court-style, box stage" and the "popular-temporary stage in a fair".'

In this context, a detailed recounting of Gvozdev's description is beyond the scope of this essay. The opera house, wherein operas and ballets are held, and which Gvozdev presents as a completed version of the box stage, is clearly a theatre style that early-20th-century directors tried to overcome.

Yet, from the perspective of theatre history, this is just one possibility that considers the theatrical space. Gvozdev, while conscious of the simplification of the discussion, describes theatre history in terms of space in a binary opposition, opting to present 'another tradition' that replaces theatre history as literary history. Referring to Max Reinhardt and others' theatre reform movements in the late 19th and early 20th centuries, Gvozdev states, 'Theatres lost trust in the immutability of the court theatre system, the material base of which has been preserved in the form of opera and ballet buildings with a box stage serving drama. At the same time, they lost the techniques of actors that grew up in the system of popular theatre. Western theatre is now standing at a crossroads'. (ibid: 35-36) He further emphasises that theatres have undergone rapid change in the early 20th century and are facing a crisis. Furthermore, he notes:

> Theatre has not yet found a way to overcome the epidemic crisis, and painful formal exploration is ahead of them as an unavoidable fate [...] Given the crucial task left over by the October Revolution, Russian theatre must build a new system of theatre for wide audiences. An accurate understanding of the historical destiny of theatre is an essential prerequisite for successful construction. At the same time, clearing the long-standing struggle between the systems of 'court' and 'popular' theatre, in which the shift of the systems is observed, as a high-level synthesis must become a new theatre system of revolutionary democracy. (ibid: 36)

As aforementioned, the Leningrad School restructured theatre history from a perspective that differs from that of play history.

In conclusion, there remains the question of the ways in which the activities of the Leningrad School may be evaluated. To this end, we must consider the post-revolutionary Russian context. Much debate concerning the place of 'tradition' in theatre art took place during that time and space. Members of the Leningrad School argued for their own theatre history and, as noted above, championed reform in contemporary theatre practice within the context of their theatre's history. While contemporary theatre practise and avant-garde theatre radically changed the style of performance, these members were trying to support their legitimacy with theory.

References

Gvozdev, Aleksei (1924): "Itogi i zadachi nauchnoi istorii teatra." In: Zadachi i metody izucheniia iskusstv. Petrograd: Academia.

Gvozdev, Aleksei (1926): "O smene teatral'nykh sistem." In: O teatre: Vremennik otdela istorii i teorii teatra GIII. Leningrad: Academia.

Ito Masaru (2020): "The Birth of Russian Theatre Studies: Leningrad School and Vs. Meyerhold." In: Slavic studies (67), Sapporo: Slavic-Eurasian Research Center, Hokkaido University.

Solov'ev, Vladimir (1926): "Igra veshchei v teatre." In: O teatre: Vremennik otdela istorii i teorii teatra GIII. Leningrad: Academia.

Projection Technology and the Theatre Stage: Light, Space, Body Politics

Kai VAN EIKELS

1.

In the late 80s, when I first became actively involved in theater, one of the most popular books among theater people was *The Empty Space* by Peter Brook, originally published in 1969. Conceiving of the theater stage as an empty space tried to moderate contemporary challenges with core traditional values of European theater. While Brook did not belong among the theater directors who endorsed projection technology (even when he used a camera and TV screen onstage in *L'homme qui*, the context was a critical interrogation of employing media in medical diagnosis and therapy[1]), the notion of emptiness he put forward sheds light on some circumstances that were prerequisite for film and video projection becoming a regular element of theater performances. These circumstances are aesthetic and social-political, as well as technological.

Projecting film or video requires that the audience and the stage are dark enough for a projection to be visible. It took surprisingly long until that was accomplished. Since the Italian Renaissance, when plays were first performed inside theater buildings on proscenium stages with settings designed according to the laws of central perspective, theater theoreticians had demanded that the stage be more brightly lit while the audience should be sitting in darkness. Technological solutions using mirrors helped intensify the stage lighting, but for centuries the audience room remained the same: illuminated by candelabras, leaving spectators plainly visible for each other during the entire performance. Even at the end of the 19th century, as gaslight and electric light

---

1 *L'homme qui* (1993) was based on Oliver Sack's book *The Man Who Mistook His Wife for a Hat*.

that could be switched off would have permitted total darkness, theaters preferred to keep the lights on slightly dimmed. In his lecture on *Optical Media*, German media theorist Friedrich Kittler quotes Charles Garnier, the architect of the Paris opera, arguing against a total blackout:

> "First, opera visitors had to be able to read along during the dazzlingly incomprehensible songs in the libretto of the current opera in order to understand at least some of the plot. Second, as a social event people go to the theater not only to see but also to be seen. (Princes, above all, were always illuminated in their boxes, because for them everything depended on courtly representation or glamor rather than bourgeois illusion.) Third, Garnier argued that it is crucial for actors and the artistic quality of their performance that they see all of the audience's reactions; they thus perform in an optical feedback loop. Fourth, a darkened auditorium would also have the disadvantage that it would not be controllable down to the last corner. Opera visitors who no longer read along in the libretto during a love aria might resort to quite different thoughts or actions." (Kittler 1999: 169)

The Bayreuth Festspielhaus was the first theater to use electric light, and Richard Wagner's vision of total immersion in the fictional reality of the performance called for darkness everywhere but on the stage. Yet, although Wagner managed to hide the musicians from the sight of the audience by covering the orchestra pit, he had to concede a certain degree of light in the auditorium. When, in 1876, the curtain rose after the performance and the German Emperor sitting in the audience remained dimly lit, this became a scandal (ibid: 170).

The process of dimming down the audience, with its delays and its – episodic – success in the 20th century, reflects the fight between two concepts of theater: theater as a popular entertainment spectacle; and theater as a form of art, a decent aesthetic discipline related to literature, music, and the visual arts. In the London playhouses of Shakespeare's era, where only the boxes had roofs and performances took place in daylight, the atmosphere likely was still close to that of dogfight arenas. Lords climbed the side stage to show off in their latest dresses, light chatter over eating and drinking continued while the actors declaimed their dialogues and monologues, and prostitutes served customers. France and Germany were at the forefront of the neoclassical fashion in the 18th century, which sought to redefine the theater as a place where literary works of art would be presented in silence to attentive, devoted listeners and viewers. Yet, the artists and progressive principals found it quite hard to discipline their audience and change visitors' behavior so their attendance matched the concepts of aesthetic perception that Alexander Baumgarten and Immanuel Kant had promoted. Some German cities deployed a theater police to make sure people kept quiet during the performance and did not disturb others from focusing on the artificial world created onstage.

It wasn't until well into the 20th century that the lights in the auditorium went reliably off upon the curtain's rise. In this period, realist aesthetics also inspired new acting techniques like that of Konstantin Stanislavsky, who taught his students to create mental images that helped them bring forth the right, seemingly 'natural' expression, and then combine them into an interior film reeling off in front of their mind's eye (Kittler was certainly right to stress the coevolution of cinema and theater, with mutual influences between them). Not only did Stanislavsky insist that actors should respect the 'fourth wall', which Diderot had recommended in 1758; he also elaborated the illusionary space so as to include passing through adjacent rooms or outdoor environments before an actor entered the stage. Set designs became themselves ever more detailed, and thanks to the darkness in the audience the setting of, say, an Ibsen play might suggest a living room lit by a single lamp while snow was falling behind the window in the room's rear wall in a bluish winter afternoon hue.

It is important to be aware of the intrinsic connection between a theater aesthetic that embraces and magnifies the power of illusion, whether realistic or surreal, and the socio-technical situation of an audience whose physical presence has been scaled down to almost zero. Those who frequently visit theaters that show plays in this tradition will be accustomed to the situation: As soon as the auditorium goes dark, the conversations break off within seconds, and all eyes are, and mostly remain, on the stage. Contrary to what Garnier had suspected (or pretended to suspect), absence of light has helped interiorize the police; abandoned in darkness, spectators learned to police each other.

Brook's term 'empty space' attempts to continue in this bourgeois tradition of a thespian art that evolved in the 18th century. His book was published in a time when a politicized avant-garde – The Living Theatre and Richard Schechner's The Performance Group, to name but two prominent examples – turned the lights in the audience back on, trying to overcome theatrical representation in favor of participation (which could include having sex with audience members or being carried by them out of the theater building into the street). The book's famous first sentence, "I can take any empty space and call it a bare stage," (Brook 2008: 7) appears to open up the theatrical to the entirety of spaces, illuminated by whatever natural or artificial sources. Its strongest implication, though, is that the theatrical is *grounded in the 'I'* – and the 'I' is not just anybody who has eyes to see a space as empty and a mouth to call it a bare stage; it is the 'I' of the theater director who professionally represents the spectator; any spectator *and* the spectator's anybody-ness, which is crucial to bourgeois aesthetics' political dimension, as Jacques Rancière (2009) has explained at length.

Indeed, the eyes of the director become like the lens of a projector here. Whatever appears on the stage – wherever that stage is located, in whichever environment it is embedded – will be a materialization of a single person's vision. It will have been produced by one man's (or perhaps woman's) subjective perception and imagination commanding a cast of actors and a team of technicians, who in turn manage bodies and machines. Projection technology had already been in use on theater stages for decades when Brook wrote the four lectures that were assembled into the book. But the deeply ideological term 'empty space' marks a point in the history of theater when the production of a theater performance is claimed to be a *visionary-technical act*. If theater is that which a director has seen, converted into images for everyone to see, then projection is the very principle of theater work.

2.

Erwin Piscator is commonly assumed to have been the first theater director who used film projection, because that is how he presented himself in his 1929 book *Das politische Theater* (engl. *The Political Theatre*; 1978). Friedrich Kranich's *Bühnentechnik der Gegenwart* (engl. *Contemporary Stage Technology*), however, published in two volumes, in 1929 and 1933, gives a more comprehensive account. Kranich mentions a number of precursors, the earliest from 1911, mainly in the realm of opera and operetta, where footage from films that already existed was employed in the fashion of a scenographic prosthesis. For example, falling rain was projected on a wall or waves were projected on the floor to suggest a river. For Kranich, projection is used skillfully when it blends in seamlessly with the other elements of the stage. Ideally, the audience will not become aware of the film as a film; as though by magic, the rain is suddenly falling, the waves are floating by (Kranich 1933: 132).

Piscator, in contrast, welcomed film as a young, innovative medium suited to carrying a progressive political message. Short scenes in quick succession, assembled through rough, clearly perceivable cuts, would open up time and space for spectators to reflect actively on what they encountered, he believed. And if they realized the artificial nature of scenic composition, there was a chance that they also saw how social reality was composed based on decisions, not natural necessity, and could be changed by decisions as well. The *organization* of film, the cross-pollination between a new technology and novel narrative forms, mattered for Piscator's political aesthetics, more perhaps than the actual projection.

There were other experiments with film projection in the 1920s and 30s avant-garde. Ivan Goll, for instance, produced a Jarry-influenced play in Berlin and then also in Paris, where the surrealists celebrated George Méliés who had made films for his theater of illusions and spectacle from as early as 1904 (the way in which Loïe Fuller used colored light for her dances at the Folies Bergère, like the famous *Serpentine Dance* first shown in 1892, also deserves mentioning in a genealogy of stage projection). Picabia, Man Ray and Duchamps collaborated with Erik Satie for the revue-like performance *Relâche*, which featured a film of the artists playing chess on the roof of the theater. In Russia, Sergej Eisenstein proceeded from theater to film directing.[2]

Throughout the 20th century, from Adolphe Appia to Robert Wilson and beyond, embracing light as an element that is just as important as actors, or even more important, has been a statement for theatrical avant-gardes to distinguish themselves from a traditional mainstream. My first example follows along that line, but in letting light become an actor of its own – or more exactly, in letting it become *all* actors except for the protagonist – Robert Lepage's interpretations of Shakespeare's *Hamlet* add a dramaturgical meaningfulness to the use of projection. In *Elsinore*, first shown in Toronto, in 1995, and in *Hamlet Collage*, which was developed for the Singapore International Festival of Arts, 2016, Hamlet himself is played live by an actor who interacts with characters and things that are being projected. For *Hamlet Collage*, the Canadian director uses a video projection on three rotating rectangular screens in order to create a permanently changing visual environment. When Ophelia drowns, there appears another real body, but only to sink into a trap that opens in the midst of a projected river.

---

2   For a more detailed account, see Greg Giesekam, Staging the Screen. The Use of Film and Video in Theater, Basingstoke: Palgrave Macmillan, 2007.

By transforming Shakespeare's drama with its many monologues into a monologic performance, Lepage stresses the already strong subjective element in Shakespeare's deconstruction of the revenge tragedy genre. A slow flow of images eliminates the 'outside' quality of the surrounding world, making it appear like a stream of consciousness (or a 'stream of the subconscious'). In consequence, nothing gets to be any more real than the ghost of Hamlet's father, or the ghost is just as real as all the other characters. Yet, as we see the visible reality sinking into abysmal subjectivity, a shift towards the objective seems to occur at the same time – and indeed, *time* seems the very medium of this objectivization. Hamlet laments the "wicked speed" of proceedings after his father's death, and even before he encounters the ghost of his father who tells him that he was murdered by Hamlet's uncle, the mother's marriage with the father's brother upsets the young man. Second to "To be or not to be," "Time is out of joint" is the most frequently quoted line from Shakespeare's most famous play.

A running clock that shows the actual time will always appear alien on a theater stage, Walter Benjamin remarks in his essay *The Work of Art in the Age of Its Technological Reproducibility* (2008: 47). In contrast, the clock seems perfectly natural in a movie, because the ficticious present of the movie action is not coincidental with the presence of the audience (and in the predigital age, film reel and clock hands moved in a similarly mechanical fashion). In fact, properly speaking, there is no movie audience, as Benjamin asserts in another text, on Brecht's epic theater: the spectators in their cinema seats do not assemble into the collective singular attendance that constitutes the audience; they are just people who happen to be in the room (Benjamin 1998: 10).

The irritating effect of the clock reveals to what an astonishing degree the 'copresence' of a theater performance depends on imagination. The actors' bodies are mediating their own physical presence with the absence of the characters they impersonate, and it is for the audience to synthesize character and actor by projecting an image of who and what and how the character would be onto the actor's performing body. We thus have projection here in the psychological sense of the word: only insofar as the audience is willing and able to align presentation (of the actors' bodies) and representation (of the characters) through an ongoing process of projection, will the play, which is but a written text, come 'alive' in the live performance. The agent of this projection is, indeed, *the audience* – not the single spectator as someone who happens to be in the room, but a 'we,' an imaginary blend of all the people in the auditorium. Whereby we have another act of imagination, which is as crucial for a theater performance to provide its unique experience as the projection of the character-image onto the actor's body and vice versa. 'Copresence' at the theater does not just consist in performers' bodies and spectators' bodies being there, casually synchronizing their heartbeats and breathing rhythms; on top of that, a complex temporal synthesis needs to take place, which is irritable because it involves a psycho-somatic negotiation of different temporalities.

Video projection smuggles a microdose of clock time into the synthesized present of theater performance, and it does so even where the projected images amplify the theatrical representation. This can be observed in *Elsinore* and *Hamlet Collage*. Mostly, Lepage uses projection as a prosthesis that allows the stage to spread out into other spaces. The river that swallows Ophelia's body is not that different from the river mentioned by Kranich. Film projection complements, extends, enhances the stage design. For Kranich's eyes the stage already was an empty space that could be filled with anything visionary minds were able to imagine, and the role of technology, to his understanding, consisted in expanding the possibilities of realizing the imagined. Lepage empties the stage even further, aggrandizing possibility itself on a scale that makes the result look both fascinating and monstrous. But the projection technology registers its own temporality within the illusionary complex. The video measures time, and given the difference between life performance and the flow of projected images, this flow comes to execute a merciless beat that pictures 'the world' as everything structured by its sequences.

In reviews, Robert Lepage regularly gets lauded as a "theater magician." Still, for all the efforts to mesmerize, both *Elsinore* and *Hamlet Collage* convey some rather dry truths about infrastructure. They remind us that on a theater stage, a video will always be counting time. Whatever it shows, one of its effects will be that of a clock, and an interesting potential of projection technology for questioning and redefining the conditions of theater lies in the alien quality clocks acquire on stage, as pointed out by Benjamin. It would be vain to speculate if the dialectics between subjective and objective temporalities were 'intended' by Lepage (and after all, 'the director' is but a projection, too: a name that allows me to attribute anything I perceive to a decision). However, since Hamlet is obviously a play about theater as much as a theater play, this technologically induced *Verfremdungseffekt* inside a capturing illusion seems noteworthy.

3.

Hamlet has become so famous because it presents us with the drama of occidental subjectivity in its excess of reflection, which obstructs and deconstructs the action right from the moment when Hamlet meets the ghost. Lepage's interpretations of the play are a late celebration of these complications, and whereas *Elsinore* in 1995 seemed quite in pace with the times, *Hamlet Collage*, twenty years later, appears somewhat outdated already. My second example, the Japanese collective Dumb Type, founded around 1984 by frustrated students from the Kyoto City University of Arts, also gained international fame in den 1990's. Thanks to an agreement with Sony, the group had access to the most advanced technology and was able to project their videos onto a huge screen that spanned the entire stage – or rather became the stage. Dumb Type are no traditional theater company but an assembly of artists who work in different fields, and while some of their collaborations were and are designed for the theater stage, others are exhibited in galleries and museums or presented on the internet.

Members of Dumb Type have opposed interpretations that try to label their work as typically Japanese. Still, they belong among a considerable number of Japanese artists who were enthusiastic about media technology and whose aesthetic approach was greatly shaped by technological possibilities. In the 1980s and 90s, music videos, which were running 24/7 on specialized pop music channels such as MTV and reached a broad international audience, evolved as a promising new format. As directors often would be granted plenty of artistic freedom and could rely on huge budgets, the music video became an experimental playground, and its aesthetics exerted a strong influence on the visual arts. Dumb Type brought this to live performance.

In *OR*, which premiered in France at Festival VIA, 1997, a hemispheric screen surrounds the – otherwise empty – stage. Giant white beams that appear to be taken from a first generation 'tennis' videogame move across the dark screen, accompanied by an electronic music score that also uses distorted videogame sounds. Flickering several times, the grey turns into a dazzlingly bright white light. The projection is so intense the light seems three-dimensional. Back to the old black, the white beams continue to make their way from left to right in steady pace, until a second stroboscopic flash of white reveals two dancers who twist their limbs next to a steel table on wheels (whose austere design reminds of hospital or morgue equipment). Before the eyes are able to catch more than a tiny choreographic fragment, darkness swallows up the bodies once more, and when the next bright period starts a third dancer is there – but then, after another five seconds break with only the white beams being visible, the third body has vanished again just as suddenly as it appeared. The other two are rolling on the floor now, and one or both of them may be naked…

The performance goes on like this, and most other stage performances by Dumb Type follow a similar structure. Gigantic landscapes, architectural and geometrical forms or decontextualized elements flash, pulse, jump, waver across the screen, while bodies engage in jerky, convulsive dance movements. Sometimes two or more images overlap each other, zooming in and out, lending a vertigo-inducing depth to the visual space. The Dumb Type aesthetic almost dissolves the human body in whole-screen patterns that incessantly oscillate between concrete and abstract, subjecting the continuum of live performance to a spasmodic rhythm generated through fast cuts. More explicitly than in Lepage's flow of images, projection here serves to shape time as well as space. And darkness matters as much as light: one might say that the ultimate function of high-end projection technology is to enable blackouts of a particular strength. As a result, the 'co-presence' of live performance itself is being sliced up as though manipulated by a video editor.

If Piscator was optimistic about the stimulating effects rough cuts would have on the audience, appreciating film projection on the stage as a technological tool that promised to help political enlightenment, Dumb Type express their political agenda through a *negative* approach to technology. Fascinated though they are by the power of video projection, the performances veer towards the anti-illusionary – or hyper-simulacrum, to use terminology of the era.[3] The visual overkill of projected images creates a nauseous numbness that makes one all the more aware of one's own body's being a solid but vulnerable, indeed feeble, physical thing. In a sequence of S/N, first shown in 1994, the performers identify themselves as just such vulnerable, physical things. Clad in a grey suit with the words "GAY", "JAPANESE" and "HIV+" attached to it, one of them tells the audience, "We are not actors. I am a man. Japanese. And gay. He is a man. Japanese. And HIV positive." In another sequence, performers can be seen dancing on top of the projection screen, which is a solid

---

3   The term „simulacrum" was made popular by the French sociologist Jean Baudrillard. See, for example, Simulacra and Simulation, trans. Sheila Faria Glaser, Ann Arbor: The University of Michigan Press, 1994.

wall, and then falling down backwards. One wonders what happens *behind* the empty space that is filled with images.

4.

"There was nothing to see at the beginning," Jens Roselt quotes a spectator from an after-show discussion in his article on video projection in German director Frank Castorf's adaptations of Dostoyevsky novels for the Berlin Volksbühne (2005: 111). Actually, there *was* a lot to see at the beginning of the performance in question, *Erniedrigte und Beleidigte* (*Humiliated and Insulted*), which premiered in 2001 after the Dostoyevsky series had started with *Dämonen* (*Demons*) in 1999: an entire house, for instance, in a design that looked like it had been imported directly from a real estate catalogue, in the typical fashion of Bert Neumann; and a screen on top of the building that displayed video images showing what happened inside the house. But even though everyone could see the action caught by the mobile hand camera – including close-ups of actors' faces, conveying details that usually remain obscure from a theater visitor's distance – those images did not satisfy the audience's "appetite for human flesh," (ibid.) as Roselt phrases it. Despite the fact that they were live images, broadcast with just milliseconds delay, looking at the screen apparently did not compensate for the inability to see the actors directly. Quite the contrary, the on-screen representation may have intensified a feeling of absence.

Produced only a few years later than Lepage's *Elsinore* and Dumb Type's first worldwide successes, my third and final example already bears witness to a time when video projection in the theater was no longer considered a 'hot' technology that would impress a metropolitan audience with its powerfully dynamic images (which is not to say that theaters did not keep trying – some still do, even today). For Dumb Type, the excessive brightness of projected light provided a means to create repeated caesura, cutting up the present of live performance by enveloping spectators in momentary darkness. Castorf's and Neumann's strategy also has its point in negating or subtracting something from the standard theatrical situation, albeit with a different twist that engages profoundly with the traditions of dramatic theater, *revising* them instead of leaving them behind. Video technology here puts theater in the position to withdraw its most precious asset – the actor's living body. It allows the performance to move the adjacent room, which Stanislavsky designed for his actors to prepare themselves before entering the stage, right into the center of that very stage. What used to be a *parergon*, an addition to the main work disclosed behind the frame, is now located at the focus of the spectators' view, where everyone is looking for the work. And the work is, in fact, *there*; it happens exactly where the audience expects it to take place. However, the visual presence has been replaced with a visual representation (as has the acoustic presence, since the actors carry microphones and their voices reach the audience through speakers, slightly distorted so the transmission process registers).

One effect of this is that the stage never appears as an empty space. It does not even commemorate the empty space of Brook's era. It looks like it has never been empty. Indeed, it seems to communicate that a stage *can* never be empty, because no space in this world can. The set designs by Neumann, who died in 2015, contributed substantially to the Berlin Volksbühne's unique style, and one of his major aesthetic achievements was that he introduced the reality of *habitation*, of living in the sense of 'living room,' to the world of live performance. Interiors have always dominated the bourgeois theater stage. Yet, for all their picturesque details, their cushions and ashtrays and vases and unwashed dishes, these domestic settings never once convinced anyone that someone actually lived there. Echoing a bourgeois worldview, for which 'the world' is but the backdrop for subjective experience, the aesthetic concepts of realism or naturalism posit that every material thing be presented as the *materialization* of something *imagined*. Even if the cushions, ashtrays, vases and dishes have not been produced at the theater workshop but bought in the same shops where spectators buy stuff for their own homes, bourgeois theater aesthetics places them in the empty space, which redefines their essence. Their appearance in that space attests to a single mind (or a fusion of minds resulting in a single decision) that has thought them appropriate for the realistic composition of a scene – not to the entangled realities of living together.

Diderot's 'fourth wall' erected the regime of realistic imagination precisely in that it was *not a material* wall. Neumann's fourth walls, which are material, transform the stage, at least one part of it, into a sphere of living together. The collective presence inside the building is still theater, actors playing their characters, but in doing so, they simultaneously participate in a living room reality. This affects acting; it substitutes manners and mannerisms for acting methods: the actors behave towards the camera and its operator in a social and sociable way, making conversation with the fact of being recorded, as it were, on top of interacting with each other shifting in and out of their impersonated characters. Projection technology, thus, does not appear as an exclusive property of the director and the stage designer. Whereas in Lepage's and Dumb Type's pieces the camera-projector unit unmistakably serves as a visionary author-director's instrument (while Dumb Type members also perform, the video manifests their authorship over of their own performance), the use of technology in *Erniedrigte und Beleidigte* socializes the technological impact, to a certain degree – not the apparatus, but some of the power video holds as a medium.

The media theorist Clay Shirky once wrote that a new technology becomes socially and culturally relevant when it has become technologically boring (2008: 105). In Lepage's and Dumb Type's works from the 1990s, video has descended from film, and its innovative capacity – to blend in recorded reality with digitally created content – at the beginning of the digital epoch only renews the authority cinema had for much of the twentieth century. The videos are presented with a thoroughly cinematic gesture. How Castorf and Neumann employ the same technology, in contrast, refers to a social normality that encompasses home recording as a familiar everyday practice. And the familiarity of recording social life turns those who are being recorded into a kind of family. Sitting in the audience, watching it all on the big screen, I realize that I am not part of that family *but could be*, wherefore not being among the family members triggers a feeling of deficiency. Hence the emotional reactions from visitors like the one quoted above, who felt so excluded that he believed there was nothing to see.

Concealing the actors' bodies from direct view and making them available only through representation during longer periods of the performance, manipulates the affective economy of theater. In "Two Myths of the Young Theater," an essay from *Mythologies*, Roland Barthes observed that contemporary theater capitalizes on the actors' physical presence because it does not entice with the virtuosity of capricious acting styles anymore. The bourgeois audience wants something in return for the money spent on tickets and the time spent on crouching in uncomfortable seats. If the performance offers neither meaning (a gullible message) nor the well-established mix of impressive acting technique and charismatic personality, the performing body itself needs to deliver the revenue. Running around, shouting, sweating, achieving a state of visible exhaustion at the end of the show, the actors redeem the audience's investment (Barthes 1957: 100-102). While the actors in *Erniedrigte and Beleidigte* are in no way stingy with physical commitment, the collaboration between wall and screen severs the experiential space that provides the proper milieu for these affective transactions. Like a semipermeable membrane, the two surfaces do not seem to let through the valuable particles. The spectator's gaze gets in, but the evidence of laboring-for-the-audience cannot get out. The narrow camera angle confines the performers into a space that remains theirs, however hard they try to bust it by exaggerating their presence.

In terms of psycho-economy, this live broadcast from a space that is folded into the theater stage generates the opposite effect of *Big Brother*, which Christoph Schlingensief famously adapted for his *Bitte liebt Österreich!* performance at Heldenplatz in Vienna, in 2000, featuring 'asylum seekers' as candidates. *Big Brother* uses cameras in order to sell privacy, intimacy and authenticity in exchange for an agreement to submit to the arrangement's cynicism. The permanent surveillance isolates the people who are living inside the container, preparing their bodies (and the subjectivities hosted by them) just the way the audience needs them to feel entertained. One could say that the very visibility to which they are exposed constantly humiliates and insults them. *Erniedrigte und Beleidigte* uses a similar setting, but the fact that the people inside the house are actors and the house has been placed at the center of a theater stage makes an altogether different situation evolve. Being-filmed establishes a collective dynamic among them, a social relation which they cannot convert into individual visual appeal, not even if they want to. "Any person today can lay claim to be filmed," writes Benjamin in *The Work of Art in the Age of its Technological Reproducibility*, considering the process of visual recording and display as a chance for reorganizing the social (2008: 33). Castorf's and Neumann's experiment with video projection, which they pursued further in many other productions, gives an idea of what that could mean for the theater.

References

Barthes, Roland (1957): „Deux mythes du Jeune Théâtre." In: Mythologies, Paris: Seuil (the text does not appear in the English translation of the book).
Benjamin, Walter (2008): "The Work of Art in the Age of Its Technological Reproducibility." In: The Work of Art in the Age of Its Technological Reproducibility and Other Writings on Media, trans. Edmund Jephcott et al., Cambridge: Harvard University Press.

Benjamin, Walter (1988): "What Is Epic Theater?" In: Understanding Brecht, trans. Anna Bostock, London: Verso.

Brook, Peter (2008): The Empty Space: A Book About the Theatre: Deadly, Holy, Rough, Immediate, London: Penguin.

Kittler, Friedrich (2002): Optical Media: Berlin Lectures 1999, trans. Anthony Enns, Cambridge: Polity Press.

Kranich, Friedrich (1933): Bühnentechnik der Gegenwart, Vol. 2, Munich: Oldenbourg.

Piscator, Erwin (1978): The Political Theatre. A History 1914-1929, trans. Hugh Horrison, Glasgow: Avon Books.

Rancière, Jacques (2009): The Emancipated Spectator, trans. Gregory Elliott, London: Verso.

Roselt, Jens (2005): "Die Fünfte Wand: Medialität im Theater am Beispiel von Frank Castorfs Dostojewski-Inszenierungen" In: David Roesner/Geesche Wartemann/Volker Wortmann (eds.), Szenische Orte, Mediale Räume, Hildesheim et al.: Georg Olms (trans. mine, KvE).

Shirky, Clay (2008): Here Comes Everybody. The Power of Organizing Without Organization, London: Penguin.

Cultural Techniques of Play: A Global Perspective

NAWATA Yuji

1. The History of Play as a History of Cultural Techniques

How can a world history of play be written? The word "play" is used here to mean a form of culture in which actors or puppets perform roles. Play can be improvised entertainment on the street, or it can be a performance based on a written text in a modern theater building. Play can be rooted in dance or religious rituals, whereby the term "play" is also meant to include such original forms.

The history of the play as a distinct cultural form has been written in many ways, for example, as part of the literary history of its region of origin, or as the history of great writers and masterpieces. The history of European theater, for example, can be and has been written as the history of playwrights such as Aeschylus, Sophocles, Euripides, Seneca, Shakespeare, Molière, Racine, Goethe, and Schiller. The history of Japanese theater, similarly, can be and has been written as the history of the masterpieces in the traditions of nô, kyôgen, ningyô jôruri, and kabuki. These regional histories can be combined and overlaid into the global history of theater. Such a history can be found in the theater section of any major encyclopedia (e.g., see Kawatake 2000).

Far less obvious than this, the history of theater has also been written as the history of the actor; this is especially true of actor-centric forms such as kabuki. It would be difficult to write about the history of Japanese theater in the nineteenth and twentieth centuries without mentioning the names of kabuki actors such as Danjrô IX, Kikugorô V, Utaemon V and Utaemon VI, and would result in an incomplete and inadequate record. On the other hand, it would be possible to collect visual representations (e.g., *nishikie* and photographs) of famous actors of the same period from all over the world and write a modern history of the play both as a history of actors and as a kind of art history.

The history of the play can also be written as the history of directors. The history of European play in the second half of the twentieth century and into the twenty-first, dominated by the so-called director's theater (*Regietheater*), can typically be written in terms of the names of directors.

A world history of play can be written differently, namely, as a history of what Bernhard Siegert calls cultural techniques (Siegert 2013), that is, techniques in the broad sense that underlie cultural phenomena. What are the cultural techniques that underpin play? I focus on the following:

- Performance space
- Stage technology (technology in the broad sense used in the performance)
- The writing surface on which the plot or text of the play is written, stored, and distributed

The state of cultural technique can define the state of culture itself at a fundamental level. If we want to analyze this intimate link, we can do so from the perspective of German Kulturwissenschaft (Cultural Science). The study of historical discourse from the perspective of the cultural techniques (e.g., types and typewriters) that both enable and define discourse is a major achievement of Kulturwissenschaft (i.e., a literary history embedded in the history of cultural techniques; see Kittler 1995). Kulturwissenschaft can be used to analyze how cultural techniques enable and define play. Although Kulturwissenschaft has focused typically on European cultural history, when we connect the history of cultural techniques to global history, we can apply the concepts of Kulturwissenschaft to comparative culture (see Nawata 2016: 9–21 for a discussion on the need to open up Kulturwissenschaft to global comparative culture). Where theater studies, Kulturwissenschaft, and global history meet, a new field of research opens up. In the following sections, I address each of the three types of cultural techniques for play mentioned above: performance space, stage technology, and writing surface.

2. Performance Space

The history of theater buildings and stage technologies has already been written, at least for Western theater, with some additions regarding theater in Asia (e.g., see Hildy 2000). The range of discussion that becomes possible on the basis of these previous studies is quite broad.

It is important that theater studies be integrated with history, and specifically with world history. World history is now no longer written as bundles of distinct and individual regional histories, but as a unified history of the earth, that is, as one global history. The history of objects can also be written as a type of global history; for example, as the global history of books (Suarez et al. 2013). The category of "objects" also includes architecture. *A Global History of Architecture* (Ching et al. 2011) is a book that outlines such a global object history, in this case, world architecture. Architectural styles spread across regions and we can trace their spread in this book. For example, the chapter *The Roman Theatre* documents that the Roman Empire built theaters in the cities within its territory, and that these structures still exist at Ephesus and Aspendos, sites of Roman cities in present-day Turkey. Christopher Balme, in his book on the mixed cultures of the dominant and the dominated in the second half of the twentieth century in various places where colonial rule had ended, points to the influence of space on performance. He uses the concept of "performance space" to encompass various places where performances occurred, including streets and Western theaters (Balme 1995: 204–206). Indeed, if we use the term "performance space" instead of "theater," we can include manifold spaces for play from different areas and times, not necessarily limiting our scope to buildings dedicated to play. It then becomes easier to write a global history of such spaces.

Can a history of the performance spaces be written as a history of human population growth and the accumulation of population in a specific space?

David Christian's *Big History* is a comprehensive account that integrates natural and human history, describes the universe from its inception to the present, and predicts the future (Christian 2018). Christian divides human history as part of the Earth's history into three phases: the foraging era (about 250,000 years ago to about 10,000 years ago), the agrarian era (about 10,000 years ago to about 1750 AD), and the modern era (about 1750 AD onward). For Christian, it is a mystery why agriculture appeared in several places on the Earth in the same period, but it fostered settlements in many parts of the world and promoted population growth in these settled areas. The development of industry, which ushered in the modern age, led to the growth of cities. How can we integrate a history of the play into *Big History*? Many plays have been created and performed in different places and disappeared without leaving any trace. A history of plays whose traces have survived to the present can begin with early cities in ancient civilizations. These cities left behind a wealth of historical materials, such as writing, painting, and performance spaces. Thanks to such traces, we now know what types of performances occurred there in ancient times: performances dedicated to the god Shiva at Mohenjo-daro, India (c. 3000 BC); passion plays of Osiris in Egypt (c. 2000 BC); shamanistic rituals in Shang Dynasty, China (c. 1500 BC); Dionysus festivals in ancient Greece (which formed city-states around 1000 BC), followed by tragedies and comedies from the sixth century BC onward (these examples are taken from Kawatake 1978: 228–281).

The characters of Shiva and Dionysus as agricultural gods (Kawatake 1978: 230–232) suggest that the performing arts were born alongside agriculture, as rites to these deities. The early history of the performing arts could be explained in the context of the concentration of the population in agricultural settlements and the resulting emergence and development of cities. The Japanese theater scholar Kawatake mentions a theory, without necessarily agreeing with it, that the god to whom the agricultural tribes of Central Asia and northwest India dedicated their arts became Dionysus in the West, Shiva in the East, and the source of the Japanese nô play *Sambasô*. Rather than thinking that the gods were transmitted from place to place and the performing arts associated with those gods followed, I would like to think that the histories of different regions of the earth were synchronized by the power of population accumulation through the simultaneous development of agriculture, without direct contact between regions, and that this synchronization led to the birth of similar plays in quite distant areas. Within a city, which is itself a center of population, a performance space is a place of further concentration of people within that area. If we connect global history with the history of performing arts, the history of the performance space appears as a history of population explosion.

As already mentioned, agriculture may have given rise to performing arts in many parts of the world without direct contact between regions. Let us now turn to the history of the spread of performance spaces through direct contact. We have already noted the example of the Roman theater. The Roman Empire expanded its territory using military technologies and brought the cultural techniques of different cities to many parts of its territory. In this way, the Roman Empire brought the city as a system and the theater as part of that system to many places. Much later, in the second half of the eighteenth century, the Industrial Revolution of Western Europe spread across the world. David Christian argues that this process was accompanied by a huge population growth and that the modern city was the space to absorb this population (Christian 2018: 90–93). Theaters in the modern city were crowded spaces in densely populated areas. It is only natural that the prevention of fires in theaters became an important issue and even became a subject in theater history research (see Itoda's article in this book). It is not surprising that Japan, which aspired to be a state modeled on the Western powers, built itself modern cities and theaters (e.g., the Hibiya Public Hall in Tokyo in 1929), or that the Korean peninsula, colonized by Japan, produced modern cities and theaters as well (e.g., Fumin Hall in Gyeongseong, now Seoul, modeled on the Hibiya Public Hall; see Lee 2017). This process continued after the end of the colonial era. In African countries that gained independence from colonial rule, Western-style theaters were built one after another (Balme 1995: 204–205).

3. Stage Technologies

First, some stage technologies related to optics should be discussed.

The application of the physical phenomenon of shadow to theater, that is, shadow play, is assumed to have originated in Central Asia or India, according to Fan Pen Chen, and to have developed in different parts of the world, whereby the "Euro-Asian steppe and the seas between Africa, Asia and Southeast Asia may have served as avenues that linked disparate shadow traditions, and some influences were probably not unidirectional" (Chen 2003: 25).

In Europe, shadow plays were often called *ombre chinoise* (Chinese shadow) because they were thought to have originated in Asia; the magic lantern, a slide projection technique documented as early as seventeenth-century Europe, was also often called *ombre chinoise* (Screech 1996, 107). However, this name was inaccurate, as the magic lantern originated in Europe and spread to the rest of the world, including to East Asia. In the novel *Maler Nolten* (1832) by the German writer Mörike, there is a scene in which people gather in a house and use the magic lantern to project scenes, play a keyboard instrument, assign roles, and recite scripts to each other. A variant of this scene indicates that the concept of *ombre chinoise* is not suitable for the magic lantern: *om-*

bre chinoise is a play using dark shadows, whereas the magic lantern projects colored slides:

> ›Ein Schattenspiel! charmant!‹ riefen die Damen aus einem Mund und klatschten vergnügt in die Hände. ›DES OMBRES CHINOISES, nicht wahr? O nein, wir sind auf bunte Schatten eingerichtet, und Nolten hat nach Herzenslust einmal in ganzen Farben auf gut Nürnbergisch hier gemalt.‹ (Mörike 1967–71, vol. 4: 92)

> ›A shadow play! charming!‹ the ladies cried in unison and clapped their hands in amusement. ›DES OMBRES CHINOISES, isn't it? O no, we are set up for colorful shadows, and Nolten once painted to his heart's content in whole colors in a well Nuremberg manner here.‹

Laterna magica were brought to Japan by Dutch trading ships in the Edo period and were sometimes called *oranda ekiman kyô* (Dutch Eichman lamps). The term *ekiman* refers to the Eichman lamps used as a light source for the *laterna magica*. In Edo (present-day Tokyo), a kind of theatrical performance using *laterna magica* began in 1803, in which colored pictures were shown with sound effects while a narrator told ghost stories (Iwamoto 1992: 85–92). The Dutch ships that traveled around the globe brought *laterna magica* to many parts of the world. Japan was just one of them. As for "Dutch Eichman lamps," the adjective "Dutch" is appropriate for *laterna magica*, serving as a reminder of how this technology spread.

Perspective is a theatrical technique related to optics, which is applied in the performance space, for example, in the backdrop or set of a stage. According to Hans Belting's book *Florenz und Bagdad*, linear perspective was conceived in an optical book by Abu Ali al-Hasan Ibn al-Heitham (965–1040), who lived in southwest Asia and northeast Africa (Basra, Baghdad, and Cairo). The invention of linear perspective in fifteenth-century Florence is well known, but Belting sees the science of Ibn al-Heitham as its origin (Belting 2012: 104–126). He also notes that linear perspective was first used in Italian theater in the early sixteenth century, and spread to England during the next century (Belting 2012: 202–217). This technology also spread to East Asia. Walls, painted and posed in the style of stage pictures of a European baroque theater using linear perspective, were built in the imperial garden Yuan-ming-yuan near Beijing, in eighteenth-century China. The architect in charge was the Jesuit Giuseppe Castiglione from Italy, who may have had Andrea Pozzo's book *Perspectiva pictorum atque architectorum* (original 1693–1700, Chinese translation

1729, new edition 1735) at his disposal (Mochida 2000). In twentieth-century Japanese kabuki, linear perspective was often used, though not rigorously, for scenery (Mende 2002).

It would be unfair to discuss only the optical technologies. Let us not leave the acoustic technologies unmentioned. Susanne Holl argues that a theory of sound as a propagating wave was developed in Europe and that theatrical spaces were analyzed in this light around 1800 (Holl 1997). The application of Western acoustic theory to theater architecture must have spread from the West to the rest of the world; this was certainly the case with the Imperial Theatre in Tokyo, which opened in 1911. This Western-style theater, where operas were also performed, was designed by YOKOGAWA Tamisuke. In his book *Earthquakes*, he says: "The vibrations of an earthquake are transmitted by waves caused by the shock at the epicenter. The propagation of these waves is in all directions and forms a spherical shape. It is the same as the propagation of sound" (Yokogawa 1891: 34). The idea that both earthquakes and sound are the propagation of vibrations is also found in the novel *The Earthquake in Chile* by the German writer Kleist, who was influenced by acoustics (Nawata 2018: 23-24). This idea was shared by Yokogawa, and may have been considered when constructing the Imperial Theatre. The Imperial Theatre withstood the Great Kantô Earthquake of 1923 (which was followed by a fire that destroyed it: National Diet Library 2016). This was probably because of Yokogawa's earthquake-resistant construction. If the theater had been built with an understanding of the nature of earthquakes, it would also have been built with an understanding of the nature of acoustics. For Yokogawa, the plays and singers on stage must have been the epicenter of air vibrations, if not earthquakes. From this epicenter, the vibrations (i.e., sound) spread "in all directions" and reached the audience. The reason the interior of the Imperial Theatre is round and not box-shaped (see the photo in National Diet Library 2016) could be because Yokogawa believed that this quasi-spherical shape would allow the sound to reach the audience evenly.

4. Writing Surfaces

When discussing the cultural techniques of play, it is imperative to consider the writing surface. The writing surface is not the subject of the whole book, but it is worth mentioning here. What are some of the writing surfaces that have been widely used to support plays?

Kallimachos, an Alexandrian poet and scholar of the third century BC, compiled a huge catalogue of the major works known to him (*Pinakes of All Those Preeminent in Literature and of Their Writings, in 120 Books*; this English title is derived from Acosta-Hughes et al. 2011: 120), including a category for drama (Acosta-Hughes et al. 2011: 122). *Pinakes* is not a mere catalogue of the Library of Alexandria, which possessed many papyri (Acosta-Hughes et al. 2011: 123), but a general catalogue of the most important Greek documents preserved on papyri. The Egyptian papyrus was an important writing medium for the cultures of the ancient Mediterranean world, including the Greek, Hellenistic, and Roman cultures and the recording of their written dramas.

Paper, considered to have originated in China in 105 AD, spread eastward to Japan in the seventh century and westward to European factories in the twelfth century. Woodblock printing began in China in the seventh century and letterpress printing in the eleventh century, with both then spreading to neighboring areas. In Europe, letterpress printing began in the mid-fifteenth century. All this was printed on paper. The *Thirty Plays of the Yuan Dynasty* (thirteenth/fourteenth century, China) were printed in woodblock, the *Kanze School Nô Dramas* (c. 1600, Japan) in wood type, and the first complete works of Shakespeare (so-called First Folio, England, 1623) in metal type, all on paper.

From the end of the fifteenth century, shortly after Europe entered the age of paper and typography, Spain and Portugal spread both Catholicism and Christian plays throughout the world. The Spanish and Portuguese also brought paper with them (we are talking here about paper in the strict sense of its Chinese origin, which is different from the Amate bark paper that existed in Mexico before the Spanish conquest). Thus, a new kind of Christian play emerged in Mexico, based on a script written on paper and combined with local rituals. Louise M. Burkhart discusses a script that has been preserved: "This new literary and performance genre premiered in the early 1530s, so impressing its audience that native historians recorded an enactment of the Flood in 1531 and one of the Last Judgment in 1533. Some performances involved hundreds of participants and included songs, dances, or processions in addition to the spoken script. Through the use of multi-level stages, ropes, and platforms, angels could descend from heaven, Christ or the Virgin Mary ascend there, and devils could drag people down into hell" (Burkhart 1992: 266).

The Catholic mission of Spain and Portugal also reached Japan. Here, too, the same thing happened as in Mexico: using scripts and devices, Christian plays were performed, blending local and European elements. In a play performed in Bungo, Kyushu, on Easter 1562 (more precisely, the scene from the

Old Testament book of Exodus, where the waters of the Red Sea break open to reveal the land allow the Israelites to pass through, then close to drown Pharaoh's soldiers), it is assumed that a stage device was used for the first time in Japan. Thomas F. Leims cites this example and speculates that the stage sets of Christian plays performed in Japan in the second half of the sixteenth century were a source of inspiration for the stage sets of ningyô jôruri and kabuki. Behind the large scale of the production, which must have been well prepared, Leims suggests that there was a script written in Japanese: a Japanese man of Yokoseura, Kyushu, known as Paolo, may have written the script, blending the European style of drama, including the use of theatrical devices, with the Japanese style of drama, and would have instructed the Japanese in the performance of Christian drama (Leims 1990: 289–296). If this is correct, then the Christian theater was received and performed with the help of paper originally from China and the Japanese script, which helped to create and develop ningyô jôruri and kabuki. Spain and Portugal moved both westward and eastward, using the cultural techniques of paper and theatrical devices to create impact and new forms of play in the American continent and in Japan.

Palm leaf is a writing surface that coexisted with paper for a long time, even after paper had spread to a significant part of the world. Palm leaf was probably used in India from BC onward and spread not only to South Asia but also to Southeast and Central Asia (Yasue 2010). Kawatake argues that India's ancient epics, the *Mahabharata* and the *Ramayana*, provided the material for Indian, Southeast Asian, and East Asian plays, and were the sources not only for the culmination of classical Sanskrit drama, Kālidāsa's *Abhijñānaśakuntalā* (fourth–fifth century) but also for the kabuki play *Narukami* (Kawatake 1978: 238–239). We should also ask what kind of cultural technique enabled the dissemination of such dramatic content. The *Mahabharata* and the *Ramayana*, probably because of the writing surface of the palm leaf, could be long stories and transmitted over a long period of time to a wide area. The palm leaf, which can store and carry more information than mere oral tradition, allows for the dissemination of a long and complex story, and more opportunities for theatrical performance. Palm leaves in the Oriya language, containing rewritten parts of the *Mahabharata* by the Orissa poet Saraladasa in the mid-fifteenth century, copied in Orissa in the early seventeenth century, probably reached Japan by merchant ships and were introduced into Japan around the eighteenth century in Tsushima (now Ehime Prefecture) (Dash 2006). As palm leaves were never the main writing surface in Japan and no one in Japan would have been able to read Oriya, these were mere curiosities, but they are a testimony to the power of palm leaves to spread across time and space.

It was the introduction of printing techniques from the West that almost ended the use of palm leaves in much of Asia in the late nineteenth and early twentieth centuries (Yasue 2010: 132–133). At this time, the French built European-style theaters in the three Vietnamese colonial cities of Saigon (now Ho Chi Minh City), Haiphong, and Hanoi, where they performed operas and operettas (McClellan 2003). The spread of Western printing techniques was part of the spread of Western culture. It was a global phenomenon that extended beyond the region where palm leaves were used as writing surfaces. Western-style cities that sprang up around the world had their own letterpress houses. Tokyo is an example of a city where theater flourished on the back of such printing houses that printed plays, which were then kept in libraries. Western-style theater, printed books (with the new Western typesetting instead of the old East Asian printing methods), and libraries (in the new Western style instead of the temple archives): this was the setting and cultural context for MORI Ôgai's novel *Seinen* (*A Young Man*), serialized in magazines printed with movable type from 1910 to the following year. The protagonist, the titular young man, visits "this Western-style night theatre, the first of its kind in Tokyo and a much talked-about rarity" (Mori 1972: 323). Henrik Ibsen's *John Gabriel Borkman* (Ibsen 1909, originally published in 1896), translated by Ôgai and printed by the Tokyo Printing Company in 1909, came to the stage of the Yûraku-za Theatre in the same year. It was the first time a modern Western play had been performed in Japanese: this epochal real event is incorporated into the fiction in which the protagonist sees an Ibsen play. The "Western night theatre" is the Yûraku-za, but the word "night" probably means that, unlike the old kabuki houses that used natural daylight, this is performed in the evening, using only artificial lighting (Kittler, citing Richard Alewyn, argued that lighting determines the length of the act. Lighting is one of the cultural techniques that define theater: Kittler 2011: 105–106). The protagonist later visits the home of a woman he met at the theater, and on his way back, he passes the Imperial Library in Ueno (Mori 1972: 341).

In antiquity, as in modern times, the writing surface has been the backbone of the play, as it is a determining factor in the transmission and repetition of the work, greatly expanding the further globalization of play. The world history of the performing arts corresponds with the world history of writing surfaces.

5. Conclusion

The globalization of play, examined in this light, did not just happen with the so-called globalization of the last decades as we now understand it. It began much earlier. A world history of play can be written as a history of the long globalization of cultural techniques that have defined and supported the performing arts from the outside.

References

Acosta-Hughes, Benjamin / Lehnus, Luigi / Stephens, Susan A. (eds.) (2011): Brill's Companion to Callimachus, Leiden / Boston: Brill.

Balme, Christopher B. (1995): Theater im postkolonialen Zeitalter: Studien zum Theatersynkretismus im englischsprachigen Raum, Tübingen: Niemeyer.

Belting, Hans (2012): Florenz und Bagdad: Eine westöstliche Geschichte des Blicks, Munich: Beck.

Burkhart, Louise M. (1992): "A Nahuatl Religious Drama from Sixteenth-Century Mexico." In: The Princeton University Library Chronicle 53/3, pp. 264-286. doi:10.2307/26403767

Chen, Fan Pen (2003): "Shadow Theaters of the World." In: Asian Folklore Studies 62/1, pp. 25-64.

Ching, Frank/Jarzombek, Mark/Prakash, Vikramaditya (2011): A Global History of Architecture, 2nd ed., Hoboken: Wiley.

Christian, David (2018): This Fleeting World. A Very Small Big History, 2nd ed., Great Barrington: Berkshire.

Dash, Shobha Rani (2006): (Japanese article with an authorized English title) "A Study on the Oriya Mahabharata Discovered in Japan." In: Indogaku bukkôgaku kenkyû (Journal of Indian and Buddhist Studies) 54/2, pp. 872-869,1324 (https://doi.org/10.4259/ibk.54.872).

Hildy, Franklin J. (2020): "Theatre Design." In: Encyclopaedia Britannica. https://www.britannica.com/art/theatre-design. Accessed: March 2020.

Holl, Susanne (1997): "Phänomenologie des Schalls: Zur Erfindung der Raumakustik in der Architekturtheorie des Theaters um 1800." In: Kaleidoskopien 2, pp. 31-47.

Ibsen, Henrik (1909 [1896]): John Gabriel Borkman, Japanese translation by MORI Rintarô [MORI Ôgai], Tokyo: Gahôsha.

Iwamoto, Kenji (2002): Gentô no seiki: Eiga zen'ya no shikaku bunkashi (authorized English title: Centuries of magic lanterns in Japan), Tokyo: Shinwasha.

Kawatake, Toshio (1978): Engeki gairon, Tokyo: Tôkyô daigaku shuppankai.

Kawatake, Toshio (2020): "Engeki." In: Nihon daihyakka zensho, accessed: March 2020 (https://japanknowledge.com/).

Kittler, Friedrich (1995): Aufschreibesysteme 1800/ 1900, 3rd ed., Munich: Fink.

Kittler, Friedrich (2011): Optische Medien: Berliner Vorlesung 1999, 2. ed., Berlin: Merve.

Lee, Jiyoung (2017): (Japanese article with an authorized English title) "New Developments of the Shingeki Through the Keijyo 'Bumingwan': Focusing on Activities of the 'KukYeSulYeonGu-Group' of the 1930s." In: Bunka shigen gaku 15, pp. 21-33 (https://doi.org/10.24641/crs.15.0_21).

Leims, Thomas F. (1990): Die Entstehung des Kabuki: Transkulturation Europa-Japan im 16. und 17. Jahrhundert, Leiden: Brill.

McClellan, Michael E. (2003): "Performing Empire: Opera in Colonial Hanoi." Journal of Musicological Research 22, pp. 135-166 (doi: 10.1080/01411890305920).

Mende, Kazuko (2002): "Kabuki butai no haikeiga ni tsuite." In: Zugaku kenkyû 36 (Supplement), pp. 17-22 (doi: 10.5989/jsgs.36.Supplement_17).

Mochida, Kimiko (2000): (Japanese article with an authorized English title) "The Yuan Ming Yuan: The Work of Dreams." In: Ôtsuma hikaku bunka (Otsuma Journal of Comparative Culture) 1, pp. 102-120 (http://id.nii.ac.jp/1114/00005506/).

Mori, Ôgai (1972): "Seinen." In: Mori, Ôgai: Ôgai zenshû, Tokyo: Iwanami shoten. Vol. 6, pp. 273-471.

Mörike, Eduard (1967-1971): Werke und Briefe, edited by Hans-Henrik Krummacher et al., vol. 3-5: Maler Nolten, Stuttgart: Klett/Klett-Cotta.

Nawata, Yûji (2016): Kulturwissenschaftliche Komparatistik: Fallstudien, Berlin: Kadmos.

Nawata, Yûji (2018): "1827nen no gentô bungaku: Sin Wi, Gête, Bakin." In: Mita bungaku 97 (134), pp. 189-196.

Nawata, Yûji (2018): "Anmerkungen zu 'ERDBEBEN.TRÄUME'." In: Oper Stuttgart (ed.), Toshio Hosokawa "ERDBEBEN.TRÄUME", Stuttgart: Oper Stuttgart, pp. 22-33.

National Diet Library (Japan) (2016): Shashin no naka no Meiji Taishô: Teikoku gekijô. (https://www.ndl.go.jp/scenery/column/tokyo/teikoku-gekijo.html).

Patte, Pierre (1782): Essai sur l'architecture théâtrale, Paris (http://catalogue.bnf.fr/ark:/12148/cb310670907).

Screech, Timon (1996): The Western Scientific Gaze and Popular Imagery in Later Edo Japan: The Lens within the Heart, Cambridge (UK)/ New York: Cambridge University Press.

Siegert, Bernhard (2013): "Cultural Techniques: Or the End of the Intellectual Postwar Era in German Media Theory." In: Theory, Culture & Society 30/6, pp. 48–65.

Suarez, Michael F. et al. (eds.) (2013): The Book: A Global History, Oxford: Oxford University Press.

Yasue, Akio (2010): "Yashi no ha shahon kenkyû nôto." In: Gakushûin daigaku bungakubu kenkyû nempô 57, pp. 105-140 (http://hdl.handle.net/10959/2641).

Yokogawa, Tamisuke (1891): Jishin, Tokyo: Kinkôdô (https://dl.ndl.go.jp/info:ndljp/pid/831442).

Contributors

Hans Joachim DETHLEFS received his doctorate from Philipps-Universität Marburg and works as a professor at the Department of German Studies at Chuo University, Tokyo. Publications, among others, include the following: *Der Wohlstand der Kunst: Ökonomische, sozialethische und eudämonistische Sinnperspektiven im frühneuzeitlichen Umgang mit dem Schönen* (Tokyo 2010). His research focuses on the evolution of Northern European art terminologies following Italian art theory.

ENOMOTO Yasuko is a Sinologist, musicologist, and cultural historian. She studied Comparative Literature and Arts at the University of Tokyo, PhD 1996. Since 2004, she has been a Professor of Chinese Language and Culture at Chuo University in Tokyo. Her research on Western music in modern Shanghai won the Suntory Prize for Social Sciences and Humanities (1999) and the Shimada Kinji Prize for Comparative Literature (2007).

HIOKI Takayuki, Kabuki researcher. PhD, University of Tokyo 2014. Since 2020, he has been an Associate Professor at Meiji University in Tokyo. His research has won several awards, most notably a prize from the Japan Society for Theatre Research for his book *Kabuki in a Changing Age: A History of Kabuki in the Late Edo and Meiji Periods* (in Japanese, Tokyo 2016).

ISHIDA Yuichi studied German Literature at the University of Tokyo, PhD 1999. Since 2006, he is a Professor of German Language and Culture at the Faculty of Law of Chuo University in Tokyo; since 2021, he has undertaken the post of the Director of the Chuo University Junior and Senior High School. Research fields: theater studies and cultural history of Europe.

ITO Masaru researched at Osaka University as a fellow of Japan Society for the Promotion of Science, Slavic-Eurasian Research Center at Hokkaido University, and Waseda University Tsubouchi Memorial Theatre Museum, and since 2021 has taught theater studies at Meiji University in Tokyo. Publications in Russian and Japanese. Research focus: Russian theater in the first half of the 20th century.

ITODA Soichiro received his doctorate in 1990 at the RWTH Aachen University with a thesis on Karl Leberecht Immermann. After teaching German Literature at Meiji University in Tokyo for several years, he was granted the status of Emeritus Professor in 2021. His publications include, above all, *Berlin und Tokyo – Theater und Hauptstadt* (Munich 2008). Current interest: German-Japanese cultural contacts, Nietzsche's poetry.

MITSUMA Yasuyuki, Associate Professor of European and American History at the Department of Culture and History, School of Humanities, Kwansei Gakuin University. He studies Seleucid and Arsacid history, especially the royal administration in Babylonia and the relationship between the royal officials and the city of Babylon. He uses Late Babylonian Astronomical Diaries, written in cuneiform and inscribed on clay tablets, as his main historical source of Seleucid and Arsacid Babylonia.

NAWATA Yuji studied German Literature at the University of Tokyo, PhD 1994. Habilitation in Kulturwissenschaft (culture science) at the Humboldt-Universität zu Berlin 2011. Since 2002, he has been a Professor at the Department of German Studies of Chuo University in Tokyo. Current interest: Combining cultural history with global history.

SEO Tatsuhiko was appointed professor at Chuo University in Tokyo in 2000 to teach Chinese history. He was a visiting scholar at renowned universities in the Chinese-speaking world as well as at the Harvard-Yenching Institute and St. John's College, Cambridge. Current interest: East Asian urban history. His numerous publications include the book *Global History* (in Japanese, Tokyo 2018).

Kai VAN EIKELS combines philosophy, theater, and performance studies in his work. He is currently teaching at Ruhr-Universität Bochum. His research topics include collectivity and politics of participation, art and labor, synchronization, time and matter, and queer cuteness. Publications include Performance Research 16:3 "On Participation and Synchronization" (ed., with Bettina Brandl-Risi), 2011; *Die Kunst des Kollektiven. Performance zwischen Theater, Politik und Sozio-Ökonomie*, 2013; *Art works. Ästhetik des Postfordismus* (with Netzwerk Kunst + Arbeit), 2015; *Synchronisieren. Ein Essay zur Materialität des Kollektiven*, 2020.

Cultural Studies

Gabriele Klein
Pina Bausch's Dance Theater
Company, Artistic Practices and Reception

2020, 440 p., pb., col. ill.
29,99 € (DE), 978-3-8376-5055-6
E-Book:
PDF: 29,99 € (DE), ISBN 978-3-8394-5055-0

Elisa Ganivet
Border Wall Aesthetics
Artworks in Border Spaces

2019, 250 p., hardcover, ill.
79,99 € (DE), 978-3-8376-4777-8
E-Book:
PDF: 79,99 € (DE), ISBN 978-3-8394-4777-2

Nina Käsehage (ed.)
**Religious Fundamentalism
in the Age of Pandemic**

April 2021, 278 p., pb., col. ill.
37,00 € (DE), 978-3-8376-5485-1
E-Book: available as free open access publication
PDF: ISBN 978-3-8394-5485-5

All print, e-book and open access versions of the titles in our list
are available in our online shop www.transcript-publishing.com

Cultural Studies

Ivana Pilic, Anne Wiederhold-Daryanavard (eds.)
Art Practices in the Migration Society
Transcultural Strategies in Action
at Brunnenpassage in Vienna

March 2021, 244 p., pb.
29,00 € (DE), 978-3-8376-5620-6
E-Book:
PDF: 25,99 € (DE), ISBN 978-3-8394-5620-0

German A. Duarte, Justin Michael Battin (eds.)
Reading »Black Mirror«
Insights into Technology and the Post-Media Condition

January 2021, 334 p., pb.
32,00 € (DE), 978-3-8376-5232-1
E-Book:
PDF: 31,99 € (DE), ISBN 978-3-8394-5232-5

Krista Lynes, Tyler Morgenstern, Ian Alan Paul (eds.)
Moving Images
Mediating Migration as Crisis

2020, 320 p., pb., col. ill.
40,00 € (DE), 978-3-8376-4827-0
E-Book: available as free open access publication
PDF: ISBN 978-3-8394-4827-4

**All print, e-book and open access versions of the titles in our list
are available in our online shop www.transcript-publishing.com**